C000271744

SEVERN'S *SOUTHERN* HILLS

*for Edmund, Edwin,
and Eleanor*

Hunt End Books
66 Enfield Road, Hunt End, Redditch,
Worcestershire B97 5NH.
First published in Great Britain by
Hunt End Books 2011

Acknowledgements
The publisher would like to thank those who helped
With the preparation of this book or gave
permission to reproduce illustrations
Hanson's Aggregates Limited, Clee Hill Quarry
Cheltenham Art Gallery and Museum
Prescott Hill Climb, The Bugatti Owner's Club
Anne Bradford
Patsy Lane
Terry Keegan, The Milestone Society, Worcestershire Group
John Lane Engineering

Printed in England by
Brewin Books Limited
Doric House
56 Alcester Road
Studley, Warwickshire
B80 7LG

Front cover: The Herefordshire Beacon
Frontispiece: The River Severn and the Malvern Hills
Back cover: Bredon Hill at sunset

CONTENTS

SEVERN'S
S·O·U·T·H·E·R·N
HILLS

Text, photography and design by
John Bradford

Hunt End Books

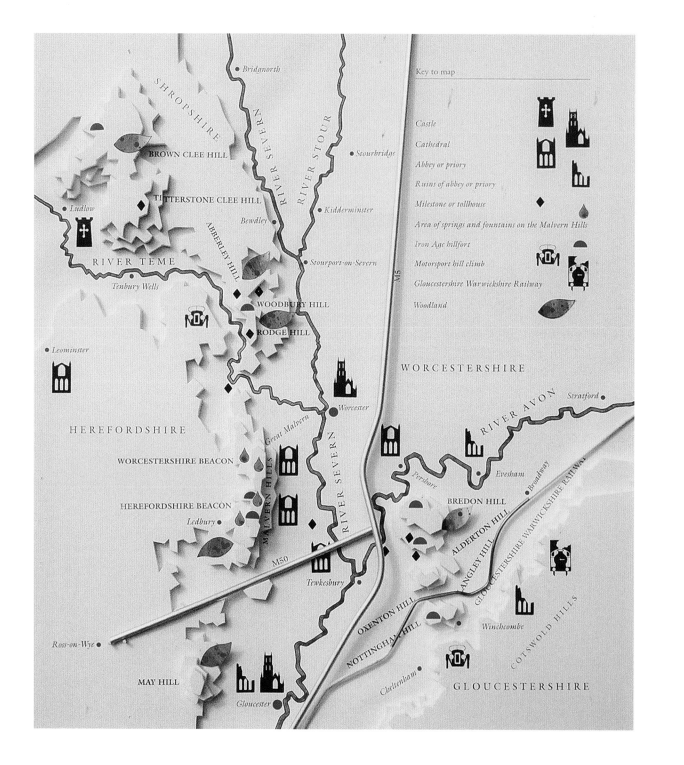

Bridgnorth

SHROPSHIRE

BROWN CLEE HILL

Stourbridge

RIVER SEVERN

RIVER STOUR

TITTERSTONE CLEE HILL

Ludlow

Bewdley

Kidderminster

ABBERLEY HILL

RIVER TEME

Stourport-on-Severn

Tenbury Wells

WOODBURY HILL

Leominster

RODGE HILL

M5

WORCESTERSHIRE

Worcester

HEREFORDSHIRE

Great Malvern

WORCESTERSHIRE BEACON

RIVER AVON

Stratford

MALVERN HILLS

RIVER SEVERN

Pershore

Evesham

Broadway

HEREFORDSHIRE BEACON

BREDON HILL

Ledbury

ALDERTON HILL

GLOUCESTERSHIRE WARWICKSHIRE RAILWAY

M50

LANGLEY HILL

Tewkesbury

OXENTON HILL

Winchcombe

COTSWOLD HILLS

Ross-on-Wye

NOTTINGHAM HILL

MAY HILL

Cheltenham

GLOUCESTERSHIRE

Gloucester

Key to map

Castle

Cathedral

Abbey or priory

Ruins of abbey or priory

Milestone or tollhouse

Area of springs and fountains on the Malvern Hills

Iron Age hillfort

Motorsport hill climb

Gloucestershire Warwickshire Railway

Woodland

Introduction

The broad valley of the river Severn between Bridgnorth and Gloucester is flanked by ranges of hills on both sides. The Clees, Abberley Hills and Malverns to the west and the Cotswolds and their outliers to the south east. Rain falling on these hills flows either directly into the river Severn or indirectly via its tributaries, the Stour, Teme and Avon, which enter the Severn at Stourport, Worcester and Tewkesbury respectively. Whilst the hills are the subjects of this book, it is the river Severn that gives the area its sense of cohesion.

About 650 million years of age, the Pre-Cambrian Malverns are some of the oldest hills in the world. The Abberley hills were formed in the Silurian period 450 million years ago, and the Old Red Sandstone Clees are 400 million years old. On the opposite, eastern side of the Severn valley, the Cotswolds and their outliers are much younger than any of those to the west. They were formed 200 million years ago and are composed of layers of oolitic limestone overlaying layers of marlstone, sand and clay.

The early history of man in the region echoes that of its geology. A number of Anglo-Saxon pagan burials, accompanied by grave goods, have been found on and below the Cotswold escarpment. Few, if any, have been found west of the river Severn. On that side of the river, Celtic Christianity prevailed, but as time went on English influence spread westwards. You do not have to travel far to the west before coming across Welsh place names scattered among the English ones. In neighbouring Herefordshire, Welsh was widely spoken at the time of the Norman conquest.

All these hills, including the summits, are accessible by public footpaths, with the exception of Oxenton and Alderton Hills, the summits of which have no right of way. Gone are the days, happily, when most footpaths were overgrown with weeds and brambles. Most are now well-maintained with adequate waymarks, although the maintenance and repairs of signs and information displays are sometimes less than perfect.

My choice of hills for this book was determined by the self-imposed limitation that all should rise above the surrounding countryside on all sides. I excluded any that were merely the highest land on a broad expanse of upland, such as Cleeve Hill, which overlooks Cheltenham racecourse and is a familiar site on TV sports programmes. Although very impressive when viewed from the racecourse, from all other directions it is merely the culmination of rising ground throughout the Cotswold hills. Nottingham Hill comes closest to breaking my rule due to its connection by a slightly lower isthmus of land connecting it to Cleeve Hill. I readily accept, however, that this selection of hills is, to some extent, subjective. Others might well have chosen differently.

For the last thirty years and more I have explored this region as well as that further west into the Welsh Marches and beyond, so I ought to know it well, but I am continually being surprised. May Hill in spring was a revelation, where the banks of some of the narrow lanes were bejewelled with ladysmock, daffodils and primroses, and the woods white with wood anemones. Another was the sheer gargantuan scale of the still-active Dhu Stone quarries on Titterstone Clee Hill, where the quarrymen and their great machines were dwarfed far below me as I viewed the scene from the quarry's rim. At Hope Bagot, an archaic ecclesiastical rule decreed in 1292 that a millstone, the cause of the miller's death, should, as punishment and retribution, be made a foundation stone of the little Norman church's tower. Inanimate objects and animals were held responsible for crimes in medieval times. You can still see it. In the far corner of the same church's graveyard, there is an ancient yew tree, centuries older than the church, which stands on the edge of a steep bank at the foot of which is a holy well. The tree, judging by the many and varied objects that are placed or tied on its branches, still attracts those who venerate it and leave 'gifts for the gods' much as their ancestors did centuries earlier. The hills of the lower Severn valley have this and far more to offer, as will become apparent in the pages of this book.

BROWN CLEE HILL
540 metres ❖ *1772 feet*

rown Clee doesn't get the attention it deserves, perhaps because, in spite of being Shropshire's highest hill, from a distance it has, frankly, an undistinguished profile. Its slightly lower twin, Titterstone Clee, has, by comparison, quite a noble profile. But as that curmudgeonly patron saint of hillwalkers, A Wainwright, observed, height alone does not make a mountain. I, too, for many years apart from crossing the hill once in the course of walking the 'Shropshire Way', neglected Brown Clee for more obvious attractions. I now know better.

In plan, Brown Clee is a figure of eight, its crossing point extremely narrow, a fact that goes entirely unnoticed from below where it appears to be one long hill with a summit each end, the highest Abdon Burf at the north. These are the 'blue remembered hills' of my childhood which I saw every day from my home in Corve Dale. More than any other hill in this book, Brown Clee offers miles of wild, bracken-covered, sheep-grazed upland with magnificent views across the hills and valleys of Shropshire to the west and the Severn Valley to the east. Clee Liberty Common, Nordy Bank Iron Age hillfort and the steep-sided valley leading from Cockshutford up to The Five Springs is particularly attractive.

From the bridge over the stream at Cockshutford, a track climbs the hill, passing through a farm gate then over a gully of large stones gauged out of the earth by heavy rain and sent tumbling down the hillside. It is a ford, passable only by off-road vehicles. In mid-June, on

Right: The Primitive Methodist church at Cockshutford.

Left: Woodbank and Abdon Burf, the highest point of Brown Clee Hill and Shropshire's highest hill.

a hot day, when I crossed this gully, it was bone dry. Where the track divides, one way continuing to follow the valley, the other heading steeply at right angles up the hill towards a house partly hidden by trees, there stands a Primitive Methodist Chapel built in 1869. I recognised chapel architecture as I approached, reflecting that in such an isolated spot it was likely to have been long abandoned, like hundreds of other chapels round the country, its roof open to the sky, windows covered in spiders' webs and its masonry crumbling to dust. I was surprised to find that it had a smart new entrance with mirror glass door and window and a new extension at the side. A little research revealed that the chapel had closed in the late 1950s and was now a holiday cottage. The modest conversion, retaining all of the chapel's external walls, seemed somehow appropriate for a building that formerly stood for Methodist values.

Walking up the valley towards The Five Springs, the occasional house or cottage peeps out from the trees on the opposite bank, whilst on the walker's side there is a cottage so buried by its trees that we might easily pass entirely unaware of its presence. On reaching The Five Springs and looking back, on a clear day successive waves of Shropshire hills are seen: Wenlock Edge, Caer Caradoc, the Long Mynd and the Wrekin, rolling back, one behind the other.

Left: Wenlock Edge from Nordy Bank.

Right: Clee Liberty Common, a generous gift by the landowner to the people of the parish.

Brown Clee has other charms in the forms of villages, both living and dead. Cleestanton, Cold Weston, Heath and Abdon are all sites of deserted villages on the western slopes of Brown Clee. Heath Chapel stands surrounded by the house platforms of a once viable medi-aeval village. It is 790 ft above sea level and was established in the 11th and 12th centuries, during a period when the climate was becoming much milder, enabling settlers to escape from the population explosion and consequent land hunger in the lowlands. All went well until the climate changed again and a sequence of disastrously wet summers between 1315 and 1317 caused widespread famine and death.

In 1327 only seven families remained at Heath paying taxes, and by the end of the century after the Black Death, the value of the rentals was reduced by one third. Heath Chapel is one of Shropshire's greatest treasures. 850 years old, probably erected about 1140, it is virtually unaltered structurally since that time. Built of locally quarried sandstone, its south doorway has Norman chevron decoration, and the ironwork on the heavy wooden door is probably 12th century. The interior evokes an atmosphere of centuries of simple rustic piety, encouraged no doubt by priests who had barely more learning than their congregation.

Whilst walking 'The Shropshire Way' in 1990 and looking for Brown Clee's deserted village sites, Cold Weston proved to be particularly elusive. Poring over the map, I knew I was near to it and asked a passing farmer for directions. He studied me closely, as though trying

to ascertain whether or not I could be trusted, before showing me the way, adding that I would find the church door padlocked due to the fact that thieves had stolen one of the windows. A holloway led up past the sites of village houses to a clump of trees at the top of the hill, within which stood the church. Closed for worship since 1981, it has since been sympathetically converted into a private house, retaining all of its external features, the only addition being one dormer window.

First recorded in 1090, Cold Weston declined rapidly during the 15th century. In 1341 the parish was valued at only four shillings and threepence, compared to £5 3s 0d in 1291. In 1341, Edward III's taxation assessors, raising money for his war with France, reported that it was a waste place, frequented by domestic animals, which had been depleted by bad weather and disease. The population had been reduced to two families 'living by great labour and in want, the others having fled'.

Abdon, deserted in the 15th century, was resettled by miners and quarry workers in the 16th and 17th centuries, only to be abandoned once again when mining ceased. The medieval church is a reminder of a once-thriving community, but it was substantially rebuilt in the 18th century.

Below: St Mary's, Cold Weston, as it looked in 1990 before restoration and conversion to use as a private dwelling. Closed for worship in 1981, this Norman church has been sympathetically restored and retains its original plain Norman north doorway and window in the south wall of the former chancel.

Below: The south door of Heath chapel, opposite, has some of the original 12th century wrought ironwork.

Opposite: Heath chapel on the site of its deserted village. Barely altered since its construction in the mid 12th century this Norman chapel is unique in Shropshire, making it one of the county's greatest treasures.

Left: The Stretton hills, a sequence of parallel lines of hills running north-east to the south-west, viewed from Clee Liberty Common. Wenlock Edge in the foreground, its steep 15-mile long escarpment is on the west side of the hill. Behind is Lawley and Caer Caradoc and further back the extensive high moorland of the Long Mynd. Lastly comes Stiperstones (not visible in the photograph) with its dramatic spine of quartzite outcrops culminating in the Devil's Chair. This is a potential earthquake area due to the Church Stretton fault.

Apart from an occasional church, nothing survives of these deserted villages, only the platforms on which peasants erected their houses. These were very flimsy structures consisting usually of either a single room with a central hearth, or a 'longhouse'. A longhouse had two rooms, one at each end of the building, separated by a through passage and entrance. One end was for people, the other for livestock. Very few such buildings survive today, none at all in Worcestershire. The cruck-constructed cottages that we admire, though some of the earliest vernacular buildings in existence, are invariably the former houses of yeoman farmers rather than peasants.

We, in the 21st century, casually assume superiority over the medieval peasant without comprehending the great range of skills he or she needed to survive in those times. A peasant must know how to care for his livestock. He was his own vet and butcher, his backyard the abattoir. He must plough his furrow and plant his seed, cook his meagre pottage over a fire that had to be lit without the aid of matches, grow vegetables in his little garden, a vital source of nourishment in times of famine following drought or a wet summer. He had to know which wild plants and berries were edible, which were poisonous, and which might alleviate his various aches and pains. Last but not least, every few years he must demolish his leaky, draughty, tumbledown home, built of little more than the branches of trees, mud, straw and cow dung, and rebuild it on a fresh patch of ground nearby. Few of us could compete with that.

Right: Memorial near Five Springs on Abdon Burf in memory of the 23 airmen, both allied and German, who lost their lives in plane crashes on Brown Clee Hill.

11

Winter and summer on Abdon Burf. The windblown trees in the picture, opposite, cling precariously to the side of bracken-covered Abdon Burf. Few deciduous trees are to be seen higher up the hill. Above, an altogether more temperate scene of small rocks in the path of a narrow hillside stream, the cause of attractive little waterfalls.

The surviving villages near Brown Clee are tiny – little more than hamlets. Clee St Margaret and Stoke St Milborough are among the most attractive. At Clee St Margaret, one of the principal roads enters a ford, not to cross it but to follow the course of the stream for fifty yards to where it plunges into a pretty terraced ravine, part of a private garden. Whilst waiting on the raised stone walkway for passing traffic, camera at the ready, I had time to enjoy the flight of a flock of swallows taking turns to swoop up the narrow corridor, low over the ford, scooping up beakfuls of water, or to catch some of the billions of small flies that hovered in clouds above the stream. A few drab stay-at-home sparrows, far less glamorous than these aces of the skies, had to content themselves with lining up at the water's edge to quench their thirst. Meanwhile, an enchanting pied wagtail frolicked in the centre of the watery road.

Stoke St Milborough was reputedly founded by the legendary Saint Milburga, a granddaughter of King Penda of Mercia. Pursued by a lustful prince and his bloodhounds for two days and nights, she at last fell, exhausted, on the site of the future village but was saved by her horse kicking the ground and the miraculous appearance of a spring of water. Refreshed, the saint was able to escape her pursuers and continue on her way. She eventually established Wenlock Priory, becoming its first Prioress.

Left: The Clee Brook runs fifty yards along one of the main roads in Clee St Margaret and is claimed to be the longest ford in Britain.

Right: A roadside cottage in Clee St Margaret beside the Clee Brook.

BROWN CLEE HILL

Below top: St Margaret, Clee St Margaret. This small village's early Norman church, possibly on the site of a previous Saxon church, has herringbone masonry in the east and north walls of its chancel, 14th-15th century roof timbers and

an assortment of windows in varying architectural styles from past centuries. The combination makes for a quaint, attractive, rustic appearance.

Below bottom: Bush Farm, Clee St Margaret.

Below top: A house in Clee St Margaret.

Below bottom: St Milburgh, Stoke St Milborough. The church's patron saint, together with the village name and the well that is associated with her, leave

little doubt about the foundation of the village on a site so strongly associated with this semilegendary figure from the 7th century.

Right: Stoke St Milborough, hidden among its trees on the southern slopes of Brown Clee Hill, with a clear view of Titterstone Clee, its near neighbour.

St Milburgha's Well, Stoke St Milborough, the site of the saint's miraculous deliverance from her pursuers. Dying of thirst, her horse kicked the ground and a spring of water gushed out, enabling her to escape, refreshed. She was grand-daughter of King Penda of Mercia and the first Prioress of Wenlock Priory. A charter granting her land, including that around Stoke St Milborough, suggests that the village was a 'daughter' settlement of Much Wenlock.

TITTERSTONE CLEE HILL
533 metres ❖ *1749 feet*

hancing upon a quarry on Titterstone Clee Hill at the end of the 19th century, one might have witnessed the noisy breaking of rocks with heavy hammers and overheard in the local dialect 'Them ston teekn sum poonin'. In translation, 'Those stones take a great deal of breaking.', the weary complaint of a Dhu Stone breaker, one of the 1500 to 2000 men employed at the Clee Hill quarries between 1863 and 1900. They came from Wales, the Black Country, Gloucestershire, Herefordshire, Worcestershire, Nottinghamshire, Yorkshire and Scotland and because the quarries were so isolated from the surrounding countryside a local dialect quickly developed that was impenetrable to outsiders.

The Clees are composed of Carboniferous rocks including millstone grit and coal beneath a layer of dolerite or basalt. The summit of Titterstone Clee once had the largest Iron Age fort in Shropshire, but it was completely destroyed by quarrying. On the hill's southern flank at Catherton Common there are extensive areas of bell pits, evidence of coal mining that was established by the 13th century and continued up to the 1600s. Coal, iron, limestone and basalt were all being extracted from the hill.

These industries attracted settlers whose cottages encroached on the margins of the common, enclosing an acre or two as smallholdings. Squatters knew that if they could erect a chimney and have smoke coming from it within twenty-four hours, they could claim legal right to the land. The rest of the building's construction could follow. Their cottages are often distinctive, put up in a piecemeal way with extensions and outbuildings added as and when time and resources allowed. 'Titterstone Clee Hills. Everyday Life. Industrial History and Dialect' a book by A E Jenkins, a man whose childhood was spent at the Dhu Stone Inn which was built for the miners, railwaymen and quarrymen, describes in great detail the industrial and social history of the hill. Some coal pits were situated more than 1,300 feet above sea level on a cold, windswept hill, that was subject to dense cloud and severe weather in winter.

Even by the 1800s there were no roads and the coal was carried down the hill on their backs by miners' wives. Richard Jones, who went to Titterstone Wake in 1845, recalled the young women he saw there, 'fine and upstanding wenches they were and well-dressed too but you wouldna' know 'em the next day with a bag of coal strapped on their backs'. By 1860 a ring of pits encircled Titterstone Clee, but by the early 1900s the pits were running at a loss.

A miner who began working down the pits in 1916 aged 18, having previously worked as a boy from the age of 13 in a quarry, later described its conditions. The cage in which he descended the shaft had open sides which, together with the blackness, terrified him. At first, he said, the conditions 'nearly broke my heart. It was warm in the pit and we tolerated our sodden clothes but, in wintertime, when we stepped out of the cage at ground level, the air was often freezing … when I arrived home my trousers were frozen stiff'.

Right: The rock-strewn summit of Titterstone Clee Hill.

Left: Originally a squatter's cottage, this simple building at Doddington has clearly been added to since the day it was hastily erected – the law being that provided a cottage was built and smoke was coming out of the chimney within 24 hours, the builder could claim legal right to the land. Many were built on the edge of open-cast mining sites. These bell-pits, some dug as early as the 13th century, are best seen in aerial photographs which reveal an extraordinary landscape of shallow collapsed pits, densely packed together like craters on the moon; They can be seen at Catherton Common and Lubberland.

Boys were employed to drag the coal along the tunnels that were merely inches high. The coal was then loaded into small wooden wagons and pushed by other boys to the main tunnel where ponies waited to haul the wagons to the base of the shaft. Every wagoner expected to have damaged hands due to the swaying of the loads in such confined tunnels.

By successive promotions from filler to pickman to miner or collier, all backbreaking, dirty, dangerous jobs, a man might aspire one day to be a foreman and so be in charge of 30 men.

The pits were eventually exhausted, the last one closing in 1926.

The Dhu Stone quarry was opened in 1855 in response to a winning tender for the building of Cardiff docks, and workers were hired from all over the country. Tracks were laid up to the quarry, along which trains ran at half-hourly intervals from early morning to dusk, bringing down the hill wagons full of stone and returning with provisions for the workers and their families. Dhu Stone is an extremely hard rock. Using 28 lb hammers it could be cracked to make smaller stones, from which setts could be fashioned in sizes ranging from 3 inch by 4 inches to 4 inches x 6 inches. A skilled sett maker could make a ton a day.

Crushing experiments on Dhu Stone led to the expansion of the quarries at a time when the sett-making industry was in decline, and by 1910 the output of Clee Hill quarries was over 400,000 tons per year. Between 1860 and 1900 Dhu stone had proved itself to be the hardest, most durable, crushed stone for road surfacing available at the time. Other quarries

Left: Radar domes stand today within a 28-hectare Iron Age hillfort, once the largest in Shropshire but destroyed by quarrying in recent times. The isolated cottage on the edge of cultivated land below is Callowgate'.

Right: Farlow Brook rises high on the eastern side of Titterstone Clee, tumbles down the hill between Cleeton St Mary and Cleetongate to join the river Rea near Oreton.

Looking west from the summit of Titterstone Clee Hill towards
Wenlock Edge and the Long Mynd.

opened during these years, including the one known as Titterstone Quarry near the hill's summit, which began operations in 1881, for which an incline railway was built from Bitterley. This railway was over a mile long and carried trains of wagons with a total load of 15 tons. At Bitterley the stone was tipped into main line wagons and transported to Ludlow behind one of two locomotives that were in constant use.

Quarrymen worked from 6 am to 5.30 pm with the generous concession of working on Saturdays to 4 pm. In winter they worked until the light was so bad that they could not see. Conditions improved a little after 1918 when working hours were reduced to 8 per week-day and finished at 2 pm on Saturdays. In addition to working these long days, most quarrymen had to walk long distances from their homes, where, after a brief rest and a meal, they began their second job – looking after the smallholding with its livestock and crops.

Other hills in the pages of this book have known industrial activity in the past but on nothing like the scale of Titterstone Clee which must once have echoed to the sounds of stone-crushing machinery, locomotives, drilling and blasting, and the cries and oaths of 2,000 workmen. There was even a place known locally as Bedlam, though this was more likely due to the wailing of deranged inmates of a now long-gone asylum. The shattered remains of quarrymen's buildings and the vast empty Titterstone quarries are eerily silent now, temporary home on the day of a recent visit to a pair of wheatears, summer visitors and very handsome in their grey and black plumage with conspicuous white rumps.

Right: Ruins of quarry buildings on Titterstone Clee on the edge of the old quarries. In the early 1900s these buildings housed powerful crushing machines that reduced the size of rocks in stages down to as little as 2.5 inch cubes, or dust, as required. From here it was transported down a self-acting incline railway, over a mile in length, to a wharf at Bitterley, 800ft below. 600 tons a day were sent this way to the wharf, where the loads were transferred to main line wagons drawn by steam engines that were in continual use between Bitterley and Ludlow.

Left: The face of Titterstone Quarry.

Right: Dhu Stone from this quarry proved to be one of the most hard-wearing and durable surfaces available for roads, and was used widely in local counties and beyond.

Right: 'Callowgate'. This cottage on the edge of the moor has cultivated fields on one side and wild moorland hillside the other.

These photographs are of the quarries on Titterstone Hill today where Hansons Aggregates Ltd extract basalt and granite. Basalt chippings and dust are used extensively in the manufacture of sea and flood defences, and for the surfaces of car parks, whilst granite has applications in the construction industry.

Above: Stitchwort and bluebells find a sheltered spot in the lane from the hillside between 'Callowgate' and Bromdon.

Opposite: Common-rush and the closely related soft-rush growing in profusion on the damp hillside of Titterstone between Cleeton St Mary and 'Callowgate'. This was widely used, where locally available, right up to the mid-19th century, in cottages, as a cheap source of light. Single lengths of rush were peeled and soaked in fat. A long rush, when lit, would provide sufficient light for a group of people seated round a table to work by. A long rush would burn for about an hour and had the advantage over candles, which were expensive, of burning with an almost smokeless flame.

Left: A yew tree, claimed to be over 1,600 years old, stands at the corner of St John the Baptist church graveyard. If its estimated age is correct, it predates the Norman church by nearly a thousand years. The Celts venerated groves of yew and oak, and far back in Neolithic times some of the dead were interred in barrows with branches of yew laid beside their bodies. The early church, like the Romans before them, chose to adopt local customs and beliefs, rather than alienate the people. Yew trees are commonly found near lych gates, and sprigs of yew are included, even today, in some church decorations at Easter. In Herefordshire it was, until recently, the romantic custom for a girl to sleep with a sprig of yew under her pillow, believing that her future husband would be revealed in her dreams.

In his book, 'A Shropshire Gazeteer', Michael Raven notes that 'Christian churches were often built on the site of Celtic temples. The Celts worshipped both water and trees, and the yew was especially esteemed'. Pre-Christian beliefs survived well into the Christian era in Europe, a fact acknowledged by a series of edicts from the church in early medieval times forbidding worship at pagan shrines, especially making offerings at trees, springs and stones.

Be that as it may, there is certainly a great yew estimated to be over 1,600 years old, above a steep bank, in the corner of the graveyard of Hope Bagot church. At the bottom of the bank, directly below the tree's roots, is a holy well, its water reputed to heal sore eyes. Hanging from the yew's venerable boughs are an assortment of ribbons, cards and trinkets, and a variety of small objects placed in the hollow of the tree; some, perhaps, being votive offerings.

St John the Baptist, Hope Bagot, is on the southern slopes of Titterstone Clee, its name both aptly descriptive and historically relevant. 'Hope' means an enclosed place within a valley, and Bagot is a modification of Robert Bagard's name, who held the manor in the late 13th century. There are many small village churches around Titterstone Clee, but none in a more beautiful location. The church's nave and chancel are of a plain, sturdy Norman construction, but with a striking chancel arch with capitals and a string course, all decorated with saltire crosses. The date of the tower is not known but the church guide draws attention to the two millstones used as corner stones at the tower's base, one of which may have been declared Deodand in 1292. The relevant Assize Roll for that year shows that a Deodand of 7s was 'chargeable on two wheels and a mill-stone in the Mill of Hope, the inner wheel having dragged down Valentine, the miller, whereby he died'. A Deodand is a

Right: St John the Baptist, Hope Bagot, and the picture below, its chancel arch. 'It is an enchanting spot, graced with a very fine small Norman church. Equally good is the churchyard, carefully managed for its abundance of wild flowers', writes John Leonard in Churches of Shropshire and their Treasures. It is indeed an enchanting spot, with the church positioned on gently sloping ground and facing the little group of old houses that form the nucleus of Hope Bagot, a mere hamlet. Inside, the chancel arch is the most striking architectural feature, with Saltire crosses round the arch and along the string course either side. The left side appears to be higher than the right, but whether this is an optical illusion, the result of subsidence or the builder's negligence, I don't know.

chattel which, having been the immediate cause of death to a human being, was forfeited to the crown to be used for pious purposes. (Deodand – that is, to be given to God).

Although the terrain between the two Clee Hills is not new to me, having gone that way a few years ago whilst walking the Shropshire Way, I confess to being a recent convert to its appeal. Titterstone Clee's northern slopes have the exposed, bleak, big-sky characteristics of northern and western moorlands, landscapes less commonly encountered in the centre of the country. The occasional shanty town assemblage of bits of rusty corrugated iron, re-used timber, discarded doors and flapping black plastic that serve as storage and animal shelters, the lonely, isolated cottage with its recluse and barking dogs, and its commons, pock-marked with medieval bell pits, all bestow on this hill an identity that is uniquely its own.

Rocks near the summit of Titterstone Clee Hill. Other than in old quarries, exposed rocks are infrequently encountered on any of the hills featured in this book. Titterstone Clee, however, does have an area that is rock strewn, some of which are the scattered remains of hillfort defences constructed during the Iron Age.

ABBERLEY HILL

283 metres ❖ *930 feet*

ome of the loveliest woods in Worcestershire are to be found on Abberley Hill, and on days when summer's heat becomes intolerable, the cool dappled shade beneath the trees is a welcome refuge. A path follows the hill's ridge from end to end through a variety of deciduous trees, some mature and stately, others bending towards the undergrowth where they create an impenetrable tangled mass. The occasional clearing where a tree has fallen, enabling light to enter, allows bulbs to flower in spring and foxgloves in summer. Although the path, steep and slippery in a few places, is well-worn, one can walk the length of the ridge, as I recently did, without encountering anyone. It has only one gap in the trees, offering a fine view of the Abberley clock tower and Walsgrove Hill.

'Woodland clearing of a man named Eadbeald' is the derivation of the name of the village of Abberley. Eadbeald is a Saxon name, but by the time of the Domesday Book, Ralph de Conches, a major beneficiary of the Norman Conquest, held this and land stretching across seven counties of England. The Norman church of St Michael in the centre of the village was largely ruined by fire in 1876, but the chancel was restored and reroofed. During the course of the renovations a workman discovered, in a crevice of a wall, five medieval silver spoons. A coroner's jury sat at the Hundred House Court to hear evidence from a local antiquary and an expert from the Victoria and Albert museum and ruled that

the spoons were 'treasure trove' and therefore the property of the crown. The finder was rewarded and a copy of the spoons was presented to the Bishop of Worcester. The Hundred House Hotel is a handsome building with bow windows, dating back to the 18th century. It once housed the court room and cells for prisoners.

The Victoria County History records that Elizabeth Walsh of Abberley Lodge, by indenture of 7th November 1717, granted Blunt's Tenement, an old house with about 5 acres of land, to provide a person to teach poor children, boys or girls, to read English, knit and sew, and any further instruction considered necessary. The children were also to be clothed except for stockings and shoes, and on leaving, given a Bible and 'The Whole Duty of Man'. In addition, the schoolmistress, elected from the parishioners, was to receive between £5 and £6 per annum. Was this disinterested altruism or perhaps, as the title of the second book suggests, a preparatory school for the training of future servants and labourers who could be taught enough to 'know their place'? By 1859, the school having been rebuilt, had twenty pupils, only to expand again in the 1880s to accommodate 118 children in an extra classroom. This expansion was largely due to the increasing involvement of the government in education. By 1862 the school received a grant of 12 shillings (60p) a year for each pupil, providing the standard of the school met with the inspector's expectations.

Abberley Hall is situated on Merritts Hill, a saddle of land between Abberley Hill and Woodbury Hill. In 1867 it was bought by Joseph Jones, a cotton baron, who on his death passed it to his cousin, John Joseph Jones, who proceeded to make extensive improvements to both the house and the estate. The erection of the 161 foot high clock tower left an unmistakable landmark in the county which can be seen from nearly all points of the compass. His reasons for building the tower are variously attributed to gratitude to his late cousin, a tribute to his wife who used to sew in a room at the top (presumably she liked the exercise involved in climbing up the stairs) and as an unmissable time-keeping reminder for his employees. The most entertaining reason given, however, is that he built it as a snub to his aristocratic neighbour, the Earl of Dudley at Witley Court, for whom being overlooked must have been a constant source of irritation.

Abberley Hall and grounds were sold in 1916 for use as a private school.

The village of Astley is situated near the eastern end of Abberley Hill. It consists of a scattering of houses straggling between the church standing on a small hill above Dick Brook, and the river Severn, a distance of a little under two miles. For such a quiet backwater, it has a rich and varied history. Its earliest inhabitants, the 'Beaker people' left behind pottery, weapons and tools. From a later age, a burial mound or barrow, with five oval pits containing human remains have been excavated, and at nearby Larford a 600 BC Iron Age village has also been revealed. This site continued to be occupied during Roman times from the 2nd to the 4th centuries and contained, among other things, Samian pottery, a whetstone, part of a brooch and a spinning wheel. A 22 metre deep well with a lining of sandstone blocks had been dug to provide the village with water.

Right: A typical leafy track on Abberley Hill along a colonnade of trees with a canopy of green fan-vaulting.

Above: Mature trees rise above impenetrable undergrowth on Abberley Hill.

Opposite: Plantations of sweet chestnut trees can be seen at the north-eastern end of Abberley Hill near Shavers End. The Romans introduced the tree to Britain and ground the nuts to a fine flour called 'Polenta'. Sweet chestnuts can grow to a great age, occasionally a thousand years or so, and some old trees develop spiralling, deeply fissured bark. One such specimen can be seen beside the racing track at Prescott Speed Hill Climb on Nottingham Hill.

Below: Abberley clock tower, viewed from the trig point at the highest part of Abberley Hill. It was built by John Joseph Jones, who inherited the estate from his cousin, a wealthy cotton baron.

Below: The partly ruined Norman Church in the centre of Abberley was replaced by St Mary's Church on the edge of the village, built between 1850 and 1852.

Below: The village pub opposite the church – a time-honoured English arrangement of convenience.

Above: Abberley village.

Above: The Hundred House at Great Witley.

At the time of the Domesday Book, Astley had five watermills, but had to wait until 1102 for its fine Norman church although a previous Saxon church may have existed. The south wall of St Peter's has architectural features that single out this church as something more than a simple place of worship serving the needs of its villagers. It has double semi-circular shafts supporting single shafts rising to a corbal table with carved heads, possibly by the Herefordshire school, that are reminiscent of those at Kilpeck. The only evidence of the adjacent priory is water emerging from beneath a stone arch, said to be part of the priory well, although I have yet to find it. The priory was founded by Ralph de Todeni who was granted the manor of Eslei (Astley) as a reward by William the Conqueror, for his bravery at the battle of Hastings. The foundation was attached to the Abbey of Saint Taurinus near Rouen in France. The church's south doorway has good Norman zig-zag decoration and the south door retains its original medieval iron fittings. Within the church there are mid-16th century table tombs with painted effigies of four members of the Blount family, and among many other family memorials is one of a girl, the daughter of Sir John Winford, with an adder entwined round her arm which vividly recalls the manner of her death.

At the time of the Civil War in 1642, Prince Rupert led his army through Astley, as did King Charles two years later. Throughout the country families were divided in their loyalties between those supporting the king and those who were for Parliament.

A local man, Andrew Yarranton, was one of Worcestershire's most important soldiers fighting on the side of Parliament, but it is for his wide range of other interests that he is remembered. He was an iron founder, with a furnace near to Dick Brook, along which he built three locks in order to transport iron ore by boat. He introduced tinplate manufacturing technology from Germany to England, and was interested in agricultural improvements, promoting Dutch land registry arrangements for mortgaging land. He also wrote extensively and was a political agitator, making many enemies with whom he sometimes brawled. This ended badly in London in 1684 where it was reported he had died due to being 'beaten and thrown in a tub of water'.

Left: Abberley Hill on a murky winter afternoon, seen from the north.

Below: Shavers End, the north-eastern end of Abberley Hill, with Woodbury Hill on the left.

Lord Baldwin's Hall, now a nursing home, was formerly the much loved retreat of three-times prime minister Stanley Baldwin, to which he escaped whenever possible. Born into a successful business family with a thriving iron foundry in Stourport-on-Severn, he became leader of the Conservative party in the 1930s and as prime minister presided over the turmoil of Edward VIII's abdication.

About half a mile south of St Peter's church, on the other side of Dick Brook, is Glass-hampton monastery. The monks are housed in the former stables of the Manor House, which burned down in 1810.

Left: Abberley Hill, viewed from the Clock Tower on Merritt's Hill.

Right: Countryside north of Abberley Hill, transformed by hoar frost. Ice crystals are a deposit formed from water vapour and can take the form of needles, scales, fans or feathers. Those who are of an older generation may remember, with mixed feelings, waking up as children in a glacially cold unheated bedroom to the mesmerising sight of windows covered in fans of this sort of ice.

Opposite: Norman corbal table and semi-circular shafts on St Peters, Astley. Because the heads are carved from sandstone, some of which weathers badly, many are in a poor condition.

Right, top and bottom: The top photograph was taken in 1999, the one below in 2009. They clearly show the deterioration in ten years.

Far right: Astley Church.

Right: Priors Mill, Astley.

Above: Worcester Trust milestone on Malvern Wells Common.

Below: The obelisk at Bredon, dated 1808, showing the distances to six nearby towns.

Milestones and Tollhouses

The first milestones to appear in this country were erected by the Romans, only one of which survives in this area. Discovered at Kempsey in 1818 it is now in the Commandery Museum in Worcester. It was thirteen centuries later that the next milestones appeared, a legacy of the turnpike era. By the middle of the 19th century there were between four and five hundred miles of road in Worcestershire alone under the control of different turnpike trusts, all responsible in law for the placing of milestones at intervals of one mile beside the roads. Many have been lost, damaged or removed, most as a result of government orders to remove all of them or render them illegible for reasons of security during the Second World War. Before the penny post arrived, letters were charged by the mile so it was necessary to know how many miles a letter had travelled.

In the time of Elizabeth I the 1555 Highways Act made it the responsibility of each parish to maintain the roads, failure to do so could result in being fined by the Justices of the Peace. This arrangement was barely adequate for local roads between villages and was no answer to the damage caused to the surfaces of busy main roads. A move to make the users of the roads pay for their upkeep by means of tolls was first put into effect in 1665 on a stretch of the Great North Road. Turnpike Acts followed, resulting in improved roads and better communications, the earliest turnpike in Worcestershire appearing in 1714 for the Worcester to Droitwich road. There were no charges for those on foot, together with other rather strange exemptions, including members of the royal family, individuals on their way to church and those transporting agricultural implements. Toll Houses are a further legacy of the turnpike era. Many have gone, but a few remain.

The earliest surviving milestones with engraved information were made of locally quarried stone which weathers badly. The problem was rectified by putting all the information on cast iron plates fixed to the stones. These were widely used until the arrival of triangular cast iron markers in 1898 and concrete T-shaped Bradley stones in the 1930s.

The Milestone Society was formed in 2001 with the aim of preserving and conserving the nation's milestones, and is organised on a county basis. The Worcestershire Society is very active, having successfully reinstated damaged stones, re-erected fallen and buried stones and replated and painted those with missing or defective plates, as well as recording and photographing all the county's milestones.

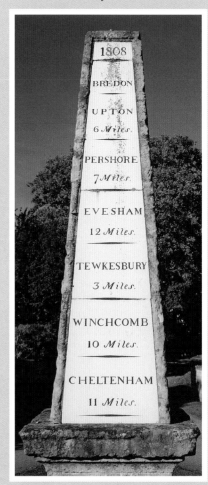

Left: Front and back of a milestone at Stanford Bridge, moved from the roadside to a nearby garden. The plate was a re-use of the stone.

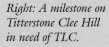

Right: A milestone on Titterstone Clee Hill in need of TLC.

Above: One of three plated milestones between Ham Bridge and Stanford Bridge near the river Teme.

Left: Triangular marker of 1898 at Knightwick.

Above: Queen Victoria Golden Jubilee obelisk at Beckford.

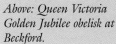

Left: Not a milestone but similar! It reads 'Shut off two horses' (take off two horses) and originally stood at the top of Broadway Hill, but is now in the village.

Above and right: Two toll houses with very different architectural styles, the one above Industrial Classical in brick, the other, Victorian Gothic in Cotswold limestone. The first is at Stanford Bridge, the second at Overbury.

A plate attached to the wall of The Hundred House at Great Witley.

WOODBURY HILL
AND RODGE HILL
276 metres ❖ *904 feet*

From the undergrowth beneath the trees a weasel darted out onto the broad track, performed a hyperactive little jig, darted back in again, returned for two encores and was gone for good. I was walking up the hill through the woods that cover all of Woodbury's higher contours, on my way from The Hundred House at Great Witley to the hill's summit, where I found an information display giving an account of the meeting of the Woodbury Hill Clubmen on 5th March 1645. One thousand 'Clubmen', humble villagers from north west Worcestershire, met to protest at the ravages of the Civil War. Their crops and livestock had been seized by both sides in the conflict, their houses set on fire and their wives and daughters raped. The Clubmen drew up a charter to be presented to the High Sheriff of the county, listing their grievances and affirming their support for king and country and the maintenance of 'the true Reformed Protestant Religion ... against all Popery and Popish superstitions and all other heresies and schisms whatsoever'.

Two hundred and forty years earlier, in 1405, the Welsh leader Owain Glyndwr camped with his Welsh and French army on Woodbury Hill. He had reached Worcester but retreated when confronted by an English army led by Henry IV. The English camped across the valley on Abberley Hill and for eight days there was a stand-off with neither side willing to risk a battle. Apart from some light skirmishing, no blood was shed and eventually one night the Welsh quietly slipped back into Wales.

Glyndwr had studied law in London before becoming a professional soldier. In 1383 he married Margaret, daughter of Sir David Hanmer, and during the next few years they were a wealthy and respected family. However, during the plague years between 1361 and 1393 there was social unrest throughout Europe, and in Wales the peasantry resented what they saw as greater burdens than those imposed on the English. Similarly, Welsh landowners resented fines imposed by the English crown and the confiscation of some of their lands. Glyndwr was declared Prince of Wales and led a rebellion. The fortunes of war favoured first the Welsh, then the English, neither side able to conquer outright. Henry IV passed strict laws restricting the freedom of Welshmen. No Welshman was to carry arms without a licence. No Englishman was to be convicted by Welshmen in Wales. None were to hold public office in Wales and 'No waster, rhymer, minstrel nor vagabond be in any wise sustained in the land of Wales'. This last order was to prevent bards praising Welsh princes and heroes.

In the north of England, Henry Percy (Shakespeare's Hotspur) announced his support for Glyndwr and marched south towards Wales, but was killed in the battle of Shrewsbury. By the end of 1403 Glyndwr controlled most of Wales. He then agreed a treaty with Edmund Mortimer and Thomas Percy, Earl of Northumberland, that in the event of victory over the king, the former would rule the south and west of England, the latter the North, while he, Glyndwr, would rule Wales. The French had already formed an alliance with the rebels and they sent a force of 3,000 in 140 ships, landing at Milford. Glyndwr and his army of 10,000

Woodbury Hill, where, in 1645, one thousand villagers from northwest Worcestershire met to draw up a charter protesting about the lawlessness of both Cavaliers and Roundheads in the Civil War. The charter was then presented to the High Sheriff of Worcester.

Right: Brookhill Court and Woodbury Hill.

Left: All parts of the foxglove plant are poisonous. The drug digitalis is extracted from the dried leaves and used in the treatment of some heart conditions.

Below: Plums and damsons, particularly the latter, are frequently encountered in hedgerows overhanging roads and footpaths in this part of the region, the juicy fruits irresistible.

Below left: Neverton Farm.

Below: Walsgrove Hill, seen from The Hundred House at Great Witley. Oast houses like these at Walsgrove Farm are a relatively common sight in the Teme valley where hops and apples were once the principal crops in the region. The orchards have mostly gone but some hopyards remain. Large flocks of geese often roam the hillside behind the farm.

marched to Milford and together, the Welsh and French armies marched to Worcester. Following the Abberley Hills stand-off the French army returned home early in 1406 and Glyndwr was pursued ever further into Wales by Henry IV's army. Glyndwr disappeared into the Welsh hills and it is a mark of his popularity that he was never betrayed. Twice, a new English king, Henry V, offered him a pardon and twice he refused. He probably died in 1415 at Monnington in Herefordshire at the home of his daughter, Alice, and her husband John Scudamore.

Sometime between 1,500 and 2,000 years before these events, the summit of Woodbury Hill was encircled by an earthern ditch and bank, the work of Iron Age people, the remains of which can still be seen although largely hidden by ferns and other vegetation.

Above: Woodbury Hill, viewed from a wintry Walsgrove Hill.

Opposite: A tree on Woodbury Hill in its autumn glory.

The casual visitor, standing in this tranquil woodland glade, listening to the wind rustling in the trees and the sound of birdsong might be forgiven for thinking that nothing of any significance, no dramatic events, could possibly have occurred in such a peaceful and remote place.

Rodge Hill, together with Abberley Hill and Woodbury Hill, completes a trio of hills separating the Teme valley to the west from the more distant Severn valley in the east. If pressed to single out just one of the hills in this book as my favourite, I might well choose Rodge Hill, although it would be a hard choice between it and Bredon Hill. From a bench thoughtfully provided on the highest point of the hill's two-mile ridge, the scenery is outstanding. Immediately below, the river Teme meanders through small woods and patchwork fields, appearing only briefly at intervals to glint in the sunlight before disappearing again between low hills. Opposite is the sprawling mass of high ground stretching away towards Tenbury Wells with the steeple of St Kenelm's Church at Clifton-upon-Teme just visible, poking above the plateau. Shelsley Beauchamp's church is easily identified below, whilst on the opposite side of the valley, Shelsley Walsh's church may be glimpsed, almost hidden among trees.

This 12th century church, built of tufa stone quarried from nearby Southstone Rock, is one of the most attractive in Worcestershire. Southstone Rock is the site of an ancient hermitage beside a holy spring, where two monks from the Abbey of Evesham lived, acting as its guardians. On the rock's summit there was once a chapel to which rock-cut steps led from the hermitage below, and as late as the mid-nineteenth century there is a record of a cottage in existence there. No trace of either exist today.

For a few weeks in the summer when these photographs were taken, the hillside around Southstone Rock resounded to the sounds of chainsaws and heavy machinery as foresters felled all the trees of the forest. It had rained almost continuously throughout July and the caterpillar-tracked heavy-lifting vehicles had left deep trenches in the soft wet clay as they traversed the hill. Although my footpath to the rock from the road, itself steep and slippery, avoided this hazard, at one point I had to cross it and, when both my feet sank up to the ankles in the oozing red clay between the tracks left by the vehicles, I nearly abandoned my plans to photograph the rock. Extricating myself with some difficulty as I continued to sink, I squelched along the tracks to slightly higher ground that was marginally less soft, and returned the other side to the path and was able to continue. The three-metre wide gap had delayed me by an hour.

For five weekends every year this valley and the hills echo to the sound of sports and racing car engines roaring up the 1000 yard 1 in 6 Shelsley Walsh Hill Climb. This is a competition against the clock that has been taking place since 1905, making it the oldest motor sport venue in the world.

To the south-west of Rodge Hill the endless green fields and woods of the Welsh Marches recede invitingly towards Wales, whilst to the north, the Clee hills, framed by the hills of the Teme valley, block the horizon. Rodge Hill's summit is a place for quiet contemplation, ideally on a crisp winter's day with a flask of hot soup.

Right: The road from Martley to Tenbury Wells crosses Ham Bridge over the river Teme and climbs up Clifton Hill to Clifton-on-Teme, which is just out of sight over the brow of the hill.

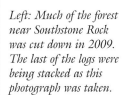

Left: Much of the forest near Southstone Rock was cut down in 2009. The last of the logs were being stacked as this photograph was taken.

Right: Southstone Rock has an interesting history. Long ago a hermit, seeking solitude, chose it for his cell. Later, two monks were sent by their abbot to protect the holy well above the rock, and in the recent past a small cottage is said to have existed there.

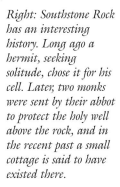

Right: Rodge Hill from fields above Homme Castle.

Left: January on Rodge Hill.

Right: The Teme valley from Rodge Hill, with Lower House Farm in the foreground, Shelsley Beauchamp, and in the distance, Shelsley Walsh.

Right: This old quarry is situated at the point where Woodbury Hill becomes Rodge Hill.

Below: Snow-capped Clee Hills viewed from the summit of Rodge Hill.

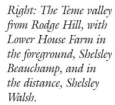

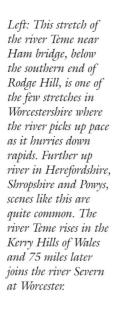

Left: This stretch of the river Teme near Ham bridge, below the southern end of Rodge Hill, is one of the few stretches in Worcestershire where the river picks up pace as it hurries down rapids. Further up river in Herefordshire, Shropshire and Powys, scenes like this are quite common. The river Teme rises in the Kerry Hills of Wales and 75 miles later joins the river Severn at Worcester.

Right: With white-washed rough-hewn stone walls, this long low cottage, together with two other houses, sits near the top of what on a more exalted hill would be called a 'pass'. This is the narrow lane that climbs from Shelsley Beachamp, dividing Woodbury Hill from Rodge Hill, then descends to the Martley side of Rodge Hill. The cottage would not look out of place on a Welsh hillside or in the Lake District.

Right: Southwood Farm in the tiny hamlet of Southwood, at the end of a lane to nowhere, and tucked out of sight below the summit of Rodge Hill.

Lichen growing on dead branches in a hedge near Rodge Hill. There are nearly one-and-a-half-thousand British species of lichen, of which 500 or so grow on trees and shrubs, the rest on gravestones, walls and roofs. They do not have roots but absorb moisture through their surface and are good indicators of air quality. Lichens will not tolerate pollution.

WORCESTERSHIRE BEACON
AND THE NORTH MALVERN HILLS
425 metres ❖ *1395 feet*

elia Fiennes, writing in the late 17th century after riding to the top of the Worcestershire Beacon, described the hills as 'two or three miles up and are in a Pirramiddy fashion on the top'. 'Pirramiddy' we can just about accept but two or three miles high would put the Malvern Hills close in height to Europe's highest mountains. Half a century later, in 1744, Lord Foley commissioned John Doherty to make maps of the 'Manor of Much Malvern' which he had recently bought. One map shows that apart from the Priory Church, the Guesten Hall, the monastery gate, and a little group of buildings, there is little other than fields and orchards. This was about to change.

In 1672, Mary Smith, a woman from Claines who was lame, 'set out to goe to Malverns Well in hope of some benefit by that water'. A hundred years later, in 1757, Dr John Wall published the results of his analysis of the water, concluding that its purity was due to the absence of any mineral content, and this was the reason for its benefits to health. As a wit at the time wrote:

'The Malvern water, says Dr John Wall,
Is famed for containing just nothing at all'.

The growing popularity of the water's curative effects drew growing numbers of visitors. Soon Malvern's fame began attracting doctors to the town who set up lucrative practices, their clients being the middle and upper classes, and comfortable hotels were built to accom-

Below: The Worcestershire Beacon, North Hill and Great Malvern. These, the two highest of the Malvern Hills, rise dramatically on the eastern side from the Severn plain. From the west they look less high. The Malvern Hills and their commons are a designated 'Area of Natural Outstanding Beauty' and are maintained by the Malvern Hills Conservators.

Opposite: Malvern Priory's magnificent tower, built in the Gothic Perpendicular style of the 15th century. It was completed in 1460. Founded by Aldwin, a monk from Worcester, the Benedictine priory was originally small but was greatly expanded in the 1440s. The efforts of Hugh Latimer to save the monastery at the time of the Dissolution were in vain, but thanks to the generosity of the small community at Malvern who raised £20 (a considerable sum in those times) the building we see now was saved to serve as their parish church.

Left: Malvern Priory's nave, with characteristically solid, monumental Norman pillars, built of Malvern stone, supports the sandstone blocks of the rebuilding that took place 350 years later. The church was greatly extended at that time, in effect completely enclosing the earlier building within an outer shell.

Opposite: The display of medieval tiles in the priory, although extensive, are but a few of the 50,000 that completely covered the floor and parts of the walls. One hundred different designs have survived, dated from before 1450 and 1500.

Below: The Priory's stained glass windows are almost without equal in the country and include the west window, donated by Richard III, mostly fragments, the 'Magnificat' window given by Henry VII, and much medieval glass as well as later work by the Victorian, CE Kemp.

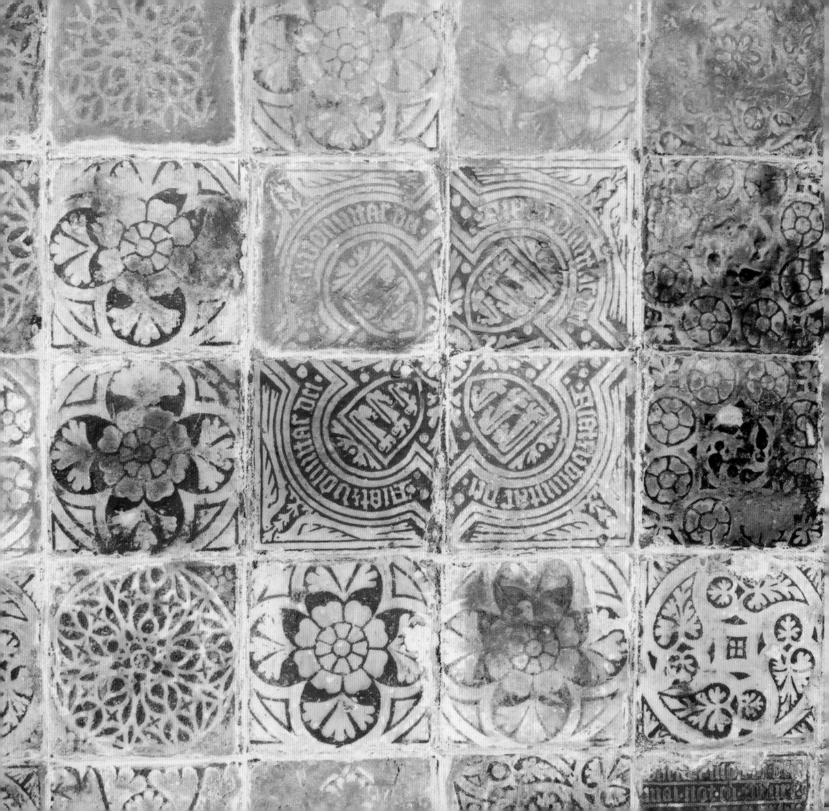

Left: The Priory Gatehouse, built in 1480, may have replaced an earlier wooden building. The entire monastic site would have been encircled by a wall so that the Benedictine monks, who were under a vow of silence, did not suffer distractions from the outside world. The Gatehouse was the only way in or out. It is now a museum.

Below left: Major restoration work took place on Malvern Priory in the mid 19th century, funded by the prosperity that came with the Malvern's 'water cure'. The work was carried out under the direction of the eminent architect, Sir George Gilbert Scott.

Opposite right centre: The Royal Library offered entertainments to the Victorian visitors of the town. It had a large lending library, music rooms, billiard tables and card tables.

Opposite Right bottom: The 16th century Unicorn Inn is probably Malvern's oldest secular building, originally called 'Le Taverne'. It was a favourite meeting place of the author CS Lewis and his hill-walking friends.

*Below: Belle Vue
Terrace in Church
Street, Great Malvern.*

*Right: Great Malvern
railway station,
built in 1861, and the
most decorative
small station in the
county. Each column
supporting the
platform roof has a
different metal floral
design in bright
primary colours.*

modate them. These patients, used to generous amounts of rich food, alcohol and a sedentary style of living, often responded well to the treatment. The remarkable improvements in their health may have been due less to the water and more the result of a rigorous regime of diet and exercise.

Malvern thrived not only as a spa town, but also as a place for retirement, with villas springing up along hillsides. Between 1821 and 1901 its population increased from 4,150 to 19,131. 'Bentley's History, Guide and Directory of Worcestershire' published in the 1830s, calls Great Malvern a 'village' of some 3,000 inhabitants. It begins its description of the town by saying that it is 'one of the most ancient, and justly celebrated, inland watering places in Great Britain, having often been honoured with the visits of royalty and being always the residence of many of the nobility and gentry, her present majesty, when a Princess, having resided here with her august mother for some time'. Churches, inns, hotels, schools, a library and newsroom are described and an 'Association for the Prosecution of Felons' which the author notes will no longer be necessary due to the introduction of the county police. From the Post Office, 'letters are despatched to London and all parts ... by Mail Cart to Worcester at 4 in the afternoon and arrive at 10 in the morning. Letters are despatched to South Wales by foot-post to Ledbury before 5 in the morning and arrive at a quarter before 9 in the evening.'

Worcestershire Beacon and its companion, North Hill, attract crowds of visitors, far more than the rest of the range, with the exception of the Herefordshire Beacon. Both are criss-crossed by many paths giving these hills the feeling of a civic park, which seems to lull some visitors into a sense of false security. I lost count of the numbers of families, with men in T-shirts and women and little girls in flimsy summer frocks and flip-flops, that I passed on a cold but sunny day in spring. Clothing that was adequate for a sheltered garden but offered little protection on the windswept bare summits of these hills.

Above: Malvern Link Common and North Hill.

Opposite: This photograph of the lights of Great Malvern was taken on Knights Hill near Severn Stoke. The town's lights can be seen clearly from the Ridgeway on Worcestershire's eastern border with Warwickshire, the opposite side of the county to the Malvern hills, which are on its western border with Herefordshire.

None of the hills have prehistoric earthworks of any kind, a fact that archaeologists find hard to explain, suggesting, without great conviction, the possibility that their very height may have caused people of that time to view them as belonging to the spirit world rather than that of man.

End Hill, a little to the north of North Hill, is a good viewpoint from which to see across Herefordshire and Worcestershire to the Welsh borders and the Clee Hills in Shropshire. On an exceptionally clear day even the Wrekin, 44 miles away, may be seen.

The northern Malvern hills between the Wyche cutting and British Camp (where, for the purposes of this book, the southern Malverns begin) is relatively less frequented by visitors

Left: A pool, near Mathon Lodge, west of the Malverns.

Right: An unfamiliar view of the Worcestershire Beacon, from the west.

Below: Colwall's church and 16th century alehouse. Puritans took a dim view of church alehouses and most became schools or alms houses.

Left: Cobnuts or hazelnuts, a common sight on the lower slopes of the West Malvern hills.

Below and left: Cradley's timberframed post office and a nearby cottage.

Opposite right: Malvern's central hills seen from Drinkwaters Farm near Little Welland.

than the often-crowded Worcestershire Beacon. The Shire Ditch is a linear earthwork that follows the ridge of these hills for much of their length. The traditional view is that it was constructed in about 1287 by Gilbert de Clare, Earl of Gloucester, following a dispute with the Bishop of Hereford. The earl had appropriated some of the bishop's land on the west side of the hills to add to his own Malvern Chase. A court case decided the issue in the bishop's favour, so the earl built a Ditch in such a way that deer could leap from the west side of the earthwork on to the earl's land, but not back again. More recent research, however, suggests that the feature is, at least in part, prehistoric.

Either side of the ridge, multiple sometimes confusing choices of tracks, pass woodlands, quarries, wells and spouts, with Holy Well being an historic not-to-be-missed example. Built on the old coach road from Malvern, the house was originally erected in 1741, but water had been bottled there at least as early as 1622, sixty years after the well was granted to John Hornyold by Elizabeth I. The present building was erected in 1843 and cleverly presents the basin and flowing spout within a 'shrine', open at the front and visible from the road.

The Malvern hills attract one million visitors every year, some of whom come to see the 900 year old Priory which contains the finest collection of 15th century stained glass windows after York Minster. It also has misericords and medieval wall and floor tiles. This and the adjacent 15th century Gatehouse are all that remains of the monastic buildings. The gardens and fishponds were demolished at the time of Henry VIII's dissolution in 1539.

The Malvern Festival, the origins of which lie in the 1920s, was established by Sir Barry Jackson. By the mid 1930s, plays, exhibitions, lectures, films and music were attracting audiences. Five of George Bernard Shaw's plays were premiered at the Malvern Theatre as well as 'The Apple Cart' which was written for the first festival.

Today, the Three Counties Showground is the venue for many events throughout the year, including the Spring and Autumn Gardening Shows and the Three Counties Show. So closely is the Morgan Motor Car Company associated with Malvern that an image of the car decorates the sign beside the Worcester Road that announces one's arrival in the town. Founded in 1910 when a three-wheeled Morgan was exhibited at the Olympia Motor Show, this family-owned manufacturing company has been in Malvern ever since. In 2009 the centenary celebrations were held for ten days by the Morgan Owners' Club, when 2,000 Morgans and their owners attended events at Cheltenham Race Course and Prescott Hill Climb on Nottingham Hill.

Left: The northern Malvern hills, viewed from British Camp.

Opposite right: A Morgan nearing its destination, Prescott Speed Hill Climb on Nottingham Hill, for part of the owners' club's Morgan centenary celebrations. Inset are two Morgans with their owners in Winchcombe after the event.

Springs and fountains of the Malvern Hills

There are over 80 springs, fountains, spouts and wells on the Malvern hills which are fed, not from deep subterranean reservoirs, but from rainfall on the hills. The ground water is held in fissures in the impervious granite rocks which prevent its escape. Water then rises to overflow as springs on the sedimentary mudstones on the western flanks of the hills and keuper marlstones on the hills' eastern flanks. The water is very low in mineral content which proved to be the unique attraction for those seeking cures of their ailments in the 18th and 19th centuries. Hydrotherapy was then the fashionable cure-all, much as fitness clubs, health spas and diets are today. Some of the springs were contained to supply bath and pump rooms. Others, like St Anne's Well, on the hillside directly above Great Malvern had buildings erected over them.

Perhaps the most striking impression left by the springs and wells is the extraordinary variety of embellishments they have attracted. Everything from a simple stone trough from which water overflows, such as Evandine Spring, to those with substantial buildings erected over them, as in the example of Holy Well. Inbetween are animal troughs, glazed tile surrounds, pumps, civic fountains, temperance fountains, clock towers, hand-pumping machines and a Gothic grotto. For those who prefer their springs 'unimproved', natural springs may also be seen, a good example being in Upper Dingle where pure clear water emerges from below a grassy bank in the shelter of a small cwm high on the western side of North Hill.

Below: Willow Spring on the Welwyn Road. In the mid 1800s the spring was shaded by a leaning willow tree.

Left: St Ann's Well. The patron saint of springs and wells, St Ann is traditionally the mother of the Virgin Mary. The well is situated about 820 feet up the hill behind Great Malvern at the end of a paved walkway.

Left: Hay Slad, West Malvern Road. 'Slad', is a Norwegian word meaning a slope or hollow. It can also be a strip of boggy land, both terms are equally apt. Queues often form here of people with water containers.

Right: Temperence Drinking Fountain, the Worcester Road, Malvern Link.

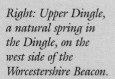

Left: Wynd's Point Spout, opposite British Camp car park. The spout is dry now, but in the 19th century provided a welcome refreshment for visitors.

Right: Upper Dingle, a natural spring in the Dingle, on the west side of the Worcestershire Beacon.

Left and right: Holy Well House, Holy Well Road, Malvern Wells. This, the old coach road, was where travellers paused to take the curative water or simply slake their thirst. One of only three wells to appear on a map of 1633.

Below: Westminster Bank Spout off West Malvern Road.

Right: Tyrol House Fountain, Wells Road, was probably a fountain for man and beast, having a horse trough above and a dog trough below.

Below: Evandine Spring, Evandine Lane, Brand Green. Attracts frequent visitors with bottles to fill from its free flowing spout.

Above: Earl Beauchamp's Fountain, Cowleigh Road. Originally the water supply for Madresfield Court, three miles away.

Right: Hampden Fount, Malvern Link.

Evandine Spring. Water flows from a wooded dell, under Jubilee Drive, to the spout into the trough. The overflow becomes a small brook flowing west.

HEREFORDSHIRE BEACON
AND THE SOUTH MALVERN HILLS
338 metres ❖ *1114 feet*

Of the selection of hills in this book, the Herefordshire Beacon is by far the most popular with visitors. On a crisp and sunny but chilly day in mid-February the footpaths leading to the British Camp were crowded with an almost continuous procession of walkers. It was the school's half term, so there was no shortage of careworn mothers coaxing along their complaining children. One toddler, his lusty wailing echoing round the hillsides was being carried off the hill by a father who was probably wishing he was back at work. Others, however, appeared to be enjoying themselves. There were also plenty of retired people, many with dogs, and lots of students. More than once I rounded a corner on a relatively quiet stretch of path to find a young couple (and in one instance a not-so-young couple) locked in a passionate embrace.

From the ridge south of the Herefordshire Beacon the views to the west and south are similar to those from the Worcestershire Beacon, stretching away on a clear day to the Black Mountains of Wales over 50 miles distant. To the east, Bredon Hill and the long Cotswold escarpment occupy much of the horizon, whilst the foreground is dominated by Castlemorton Common.

This common was formerly part of the Forest of Malvern which included all of the Malvern hills, part of east Herefordshire and part of north-west Gloucestershire. Like other forests in the Midlands including Cannock, Kinver, Wyre, Ombersley, Feckenham and

Arden, it was subject to forest law. This law, instituted by William the Conqueror, reserved and protected woodland or scrub and all game, mainly wild boar and the three types of native deer, which only the king and those authorised by him could hunt. By the time of the reign of Henry II almost a third of the country was subject to forest law, causing increasing resentment in all levels of society. Indeed, when King John, Henry II's son, was forced by the barons to sign the Magna Carta it included a clause preventing further expansion of forest law.

If a king sold or gave away part of a forest it became a chase, so in 1290, when part of the Forest of Malvern was granted to Gilbert de Clare, Earl of Gloucester, on the occasion of his marriage to the daughter of Edward I, it became Malvern Chase. Kings in need of money, much like governments today, were always looking for ways of raising cash that did not cause a rebellion. One was to issue licences to impark or assart for farmland, often to ecclesiastical bodies, resulting in patches of forest clearance round small priories or abbeys. Gradually, the use and appearance of the countryside altered as more and more of it came under cultivation. Castlemorton Common is a reminder of how large swathes of England once looked.

Left: The view from British Camp along the Shire Ditch towards Hangman's Hill, where those who offended against Forest Law in medieval times are said to have been hanged.

Right: Castlemorton Common, a rare survival of a medieval Forest Law landscape.

Left: Pussy willow. The male catkins of this common bush, which appear from January to March, were called 'goslings', due to their colour and furry texture which resembles newly hatched geese.

Below: British Camp silhouetted against a winter sun and viewed from snow-covered Pinnacle Hill.

Right: Herefordshire Beacon from Hillend Court near Castlemorton.

Right: Thunder clouds mass above the 17metre high obelisk overlooking Eastnor Park. It was erected in 1812 by the first Lord Somers as a memorial to his son who died in the Peninsular war.

Below: Looking west from the earthworks of British Camp.

The Benedictine priory at Little Malvern and Priors Hall, now called
Little Malvern Court.

Herefordshire Beacon from Pinnacle Hill.

Tucked into the hillside, clearly visible from British Camp, is Little Malvern Priory, established in 1125 for Benedictines. It was never large, having a maximum of twelve monks in its best years. Its mother house was at Worcester, where the prior had authority over Little Malvern and could discipline the monks and appoint their prior. In 1480, Bishop Alcock, visiting little Malvern and shocked by the general decay and lax habits of the brothers, dismissed the prior and his monks to Gloucester Abbey where they spent two years in a place of correction. In the meantime, the bishop had the buildings repaired, following which the chastened monks were allowed to return. A century earlier, William Langland in 'Piers Plowman', a poem set in the Malvern Hills, had condemned friars for 'preaching to the people for what they could get'.

Following the Dissolution of the Monasteries, the only part of the priory to survive was the choir of the church, which was reserved for use by the parishioners, and the medieval house next to it called Prior's Hall, now known as Little Malvern Court.

The Malvern hills have two large Iron Age hill forts, one on the Herefordshire Beacon and one on Midsummer Hill. Of the two, the latter attracts fewer visitors. I passed only one woman, a man and two dogs on my visit, - it was, however, a day of ferocious March winds which may have had something to do with it.

There is no easy way to the top of Raggedstone Hill, which, at only 836 feet, is not very high but is steep on all sides. It is the penultimate hill at the quiet, southern end of the Malverns, where woods echo to the drumming of woodpeckers and buzzards circle above the hill's twin peaks. A gem of a hill and well worth the effort of climbing.

The Reverend Symonds BA was Rector of Pendock from 1845 to 1877 and he claimed to have found a bundle of papers in the attic of one of his parishioners, giving the story of the shadow of Raggedstone Hill. A monk from Little Malvern Priory married a relative to save her from an unwilling marriage, but consequently broke his vow of chastity. He also became involved in a family feud. As penance he was ordered to climb up Raggedstone Hill every day on his hands and knees. After a year, he was so weak that he died on its summit but with his last words he made the following curse: 'My curse be on thee, thou heaven blasting hill, and on those which laid this burden on me and all that be like as they are … May thy shadow and my shadow never cease to fall upon them'. Those who have been unlucky enough to experience the shadow of Raggedstone Hill include the Prior of Malvern, who died soon afterwards, Sir John Oldcastle, a priest who was burned at Smithfield, and Cardinal Wolsey, who failed to persuade the Pope to annul Henry VIII's marriage to Catherine of Aragon.

A less implausible explanation of the origin concerns a dispute over land between the monks of Little Malvern Priory and Sir John Nanfan of Birtsmorton. Nanfan enclosed land believed by the monks to belong to them. One day he saw a monk on Raggedstone Hill and ordered him off. A heated exchange followed ending with the monk pronouncing excommunication and the prophecy that when the shadow of the hill fell on Birtsmorton Court the oldest son of the house would die within a year. Nanfan's eldest son duly obliged. Over the years the unexpected deaths of some Nanfan heirs have tended to reinforce the authenticity of the curse, and the deaths of other victims, including that of Cardinal Wolsey, who was said to have fallen asleep in the garden of Birtsmorton Court on the one day in November during a whole year when the sun is sufficiently low to cast a shadow long enough to reach the court's garden. My own scepticism concerns the distance involved, it is over two miles from Little Malvern Priory to the foot of Raggestone Hill. I wonder whether the monk would have had enough time during the day to crawl there and back, let alone get to the top of the hill. Climbing it in the conventional manner left me frequently pausing to regain my breath.

Opposite and right. Raggedstone Rock, the instrument of a monk's curse and the destination of his daily penance for his sins – crawling to the hill's summit.

Right: The white-leaved oak, from which the hamlet gets its name, is no longer there, but there are no shortages of the familiar kind of oaks in the vicinity.

Chase End Hill, a diminutive fullstop at the end of the Malverns is reached via the pretty hamlet of White-leaved Oak, so named after a tree of that description that once grew there. The village nestles in a gap between the two hills and enjoys the distinction of being the meeting point of three counties; Herefordshire, Gloucestershire and Worcestershire. The sweeping panorama from the Ordnance Survey trigonometry point at the top of the hill includes May Hill to the South, the Cotswolds and Bredon Hill in the east, and to the west, nearby, is the attractive well-wooded gently undulating landscape between the Malvern hills and Eastnor Castle.

Right: A benign looking Raggedstone Hill with the village of White-leaved Oak below, photographed from Chase End Hill.

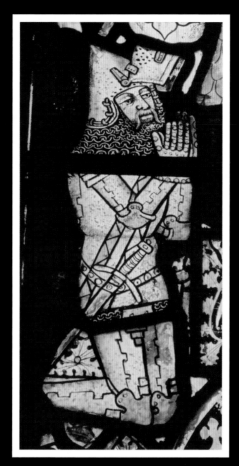

*The baptism of St Christopher, a rare
representation of this saint. It can be seen
in the south window of the chancel
of St Thomas of Canterbury with St Peter
and St Paul, Birtsmorton, together with
other fragments of 14th and 15th century
stained glass. The fine-looking
timber-framed house next to it is
Birtsmorton Court,
home of the Nanfan family.*

A cottage at White-leaved Oak in early spring.

Iron Age Hillforts

Many of the hills featured in this book have Iron Age hillforts. They are to be found on Brown Clee, Woodbury Hill, the Herefordshire Beacon and Midsummer Hill in the Malverns, Nottingham Hill and Bredon Hill. Others have been eradicated by subsequent developments, most notably that on Titterstone Clee which was once one of the largest in the country. Most were built between about 600 BC and 100 BC. Speculation continues as to the exact uses of hillforts. Most were probably at some time defensive fortifications but many have been found to have remains within the ramparts of substantial numbers of buildings.

British Camp is one of Britain's most impressive Iron Age hillforts. Its earthworks swirl around the contours of the Herefordshire Beacon and the neighbouring Millennium Hill. The oldest part, the flattened summit, may date from the late Bronze Age but most of it is from about 400 BC and later. Unusually, British Camp has four entrances, and within the protection of its ramparts 118 possible circular building platforms have been identified. The summit, it is thought, was modified in the 12th century AD when a Norman motte and bailey was built.

The Malverns have a second hillfort on Midsummer Hill which is highly unusual inasmuch as it occupies the tops of adjacent hills, Midsummer Hill and Hollybush Hill, and between the two is a spring from which a rivulet of water tumbles down a wooded ravine. Within the fortifications, archaeologists have identified 483 house platforms, most circular and some with yards and gardens. Perhaps as many as 1,500 people were living there 2,000 years ago! It remains unclear whether they lived inside the fortifications all year round or only temporarily and if so, why. The earthworks have a North Gate and a South Gate and

Left: The earthworks of British Camp swirling round Herefordshire Beacon.

excavations of the latter reveal that it had 17 successive wooden gateways, flanked by stonebuilt guard houses that were maintained throughout the last 450 years of its existence. The fort was destroyed at the time of the Roman invasion, around 50 AD.

Nordy Bank hillfort on a spur off the lower slopes of Brown Clee Hill occupies a commanding position overlooking the hills and valleys to the west. It has a single bank and rock-cut ditch and is well-preserved except for a few places where small-scale quarrying has left gaps in the bank. The summits of Abdon Burf and Clee Burf once had hillforts which have been lost due to quarrying in the recent past.

In Worcestershire, Kemerton Camp at the summit of Bredon Hill has an impressive system of banks and ditches. The outer line of earthworks, dating probably from the fourth century BC is the earlier, the inner massive defences being added later. At least one savage battle took place here, evidence for which came to light with the discovery of about fifty skeletons in a ditch. They had been hacked to death by sword. Less well known, and certainly less visited, Conderton hillfort is sited on a spur of Bredon Hill above Conderton village. Built in two phases, the earlier 5th century enclosure of approximately 3 acres was most likely a corral for cattle. Within it, at one end, about two-thirds of the area was enclosed in the 4th century and filled with about a dozen buildings and storage pits.

Below: Conderton Camp is on a spur of Bredon Hill above the village of Conderton.

*Above: Nordy Bank, an
Iron Age Hillfort on Brown Clee hill.*

Above: British Camp viewed from the south.

*Below: Kemerton Camp
on the summit of Bredon Hill.*

Sunset over Kemerton Camp, Bredon Hill, showing part of the inner fortifications.

MAY HILL

296 metres ❖ *971 feet*

ere it not for the small copse of fir trees planted on the summit of dome-shaped May Hill, its profile would be unremarkable. Planted in 1888 to commemorate Queen Victoria's Jubilee, from a distance the hill's silhouette is a little startling, an example of unintended consequences.

As March turned to April, I sat a short way from the copse within which a pony with her foal stood, as motionless as the trees. The grassy ledge on which I made myself comfortable was near to a great number of holes, some quite large, probably made by badgers. At the entrance to each hole a spoil heap of very sandy earth had been thrown out and this seemed to be an attraction for a little flock of meadow pipits fluttering about the hillside, picking up insects. In the far distance, beyond the Forest of Dean, Blorenge, the Sugar Loaf and the long plateau of the Black Mountains of Wales lined the horizon, a deeper blue than that of the sky. For those who climb hills for the view, May Hill amply rewards expectations, particularly as a vantage point from which to look down at the serpentine meanderings of the tidal river Severn. The Malvern hills and Bredon Hill lie to the north, while the Cotswold escarpment sweeps along the eastern skyline.

My journey to May Hill took me along narrow winding lanes with banks full of many kinds of wild flowers. Daffodils, of course, this part of the Forest of Dean is famous for

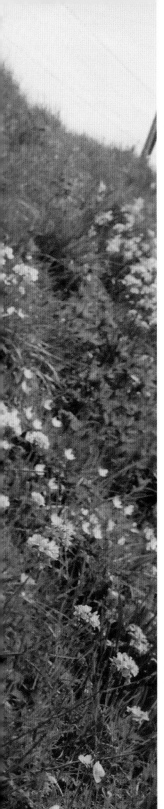

Left: Daffodils, ladysmock and wood anemones beside a quiet lane at the foot of May Hill. The daffodil grows 'almost everywhere through England' wrote John Gerard in the 16th century. Today extensive colonies of the plant can be seen in the Herefordshire-Gloucestershire border and in Devon. Elsewhere it appears in smaller colonies, but it has gone from most of the country. Ladysmock has the most delicate shade of pink, almost white, flowers and likes damp ditches and meadows, where sometimes it grows in profusion. It is one of the delights of spring.

Right top: Primroses, here seen with celandine, are widely regarded as the first true flower of spring and are consequently held in great affection. The plant gave rise to many folk customs, among which, during the times when witchcraft was greatly feared, it was the practice in the New Forest on May Day to lay bunches of primroses on the floor of cowsheds to protect cattle from witches.

those. They fill the woods, meadows and every scrap of uncultivated land. But also primroses, white violets, wood anemones and ladysmock, the last in great profusion. My guess is that this relatively small forgotten bit of countryside somehow managed to escape the assault of pesticides and fertilisers inflicted on the rest of the country in recent decades and therefore looks much as it did to generations long gone. One could become very embittered about the way we have been robbed of our wildlife by big agriculture, governments and agri-chemical companies.

Although 'May Hill' is the most widely used name of the hill, it was also known as Yartleton Hill, the assertion being that it acquired the present name from the May Day celebrations held on its summit. An early 19th century writer noted that two 'armies' of youths, one dressed as 'winter', the other as 'spring', engaged in a mock battle, always won by 'spring'. They then all proceed off the hill triumphantly carrying branches of greenery and May blossom, singing 'We have brought the summer home'.

May Hill has a remarkable reputation for stories of hidden tunnels, buried treasure, witchcraft and religious persecution.

Two tunnels are believed to exist, one at Great Cugley Farm, about a mile and a half from May Hill, the other on the top of the hill. The tunnel at the farm was authenticated by Stephen Ballard, an engineer, in 1834. He described it as having a spacious entrance from which a small underground passage led, clearly man-made from the tool marks on the walls. Fifty years later, horses passing overhead caused the collapse of the roof and again the tunnel was verified by a visitor. The cave on the hill's top is less reliably documented but is believed to be about 500 metres south east of the summit.

Left: Wood anemones are slow to colonise so are a good indicator of ancient woodland. Although this is their preferred habitat, the flowers will only open fully in sunshine, hence their early appearances before the trees are in leaf.

Mary Mayo, an elderly Newent widow, interviewed in 1884 by the local naturalist, G H Piper, said she had often, as a child, played at the foot of the May Hill cave's fifteen steps. Both her grandfathers, she said, had explored the cave and its tunnel, which they believed was connected to the cave at Great Cugly Farm. Midway along they found a chest full of treasure but an impassable stream blocked their way and, dropping their last candle, they fearfully groped their way back in total darkness. Folk stories have a habit of becoming ever more fanciful as they are retold, and the notoriety of May Hill's caves attracted many visitors, including a disbanded soldier named Fairfax, who arrived from London, intent on discovering the cave's hidden treasure, of course without success. Finally, a drunk was found dead in there, causing a sudden loss of interest.

In the 16th century, an age of religious persecutions, Catholic Queen Mary decreed that the nation must revert to the old faith. Two local Protestant men, Horne and Crockett, used the cave to hide from the agents of the state, but were discovered. The fate of Crockett is unknown but Horne was arrested and thrown into jail. He escaped and succeeded in safely reaching his home, where he was concealed by his wife. She gave birth to a son and at the baptismal celebrations she tried to secretly take some of the food to her husband, but was noticed doing so by a midwife, who became suspicious and demanded that the house be searched. Horne was discovered and condemned to be burned at the stake, where it was recorded that he sang the 146th psalm until his lips burned away.

May Hill had its witch, Ellen Hayward. She was a herbalist and a dresser of sores and wounds, in other words, a 'wise-woman'. In 1905 a local man, John Market, asked her to find £50 that was missing from his house. Within a week several members of his family became mentally deranged, one attempting suicide. Neighbours attributed this to the work of Ellen and swore she was a witch, a charge Ellen repudiated in print by sending a letter to

Opposite: The view from May Hill into Wales and the Black Mountains. Hay Bluff escarpment is on the right of the photograph and Sugar Loaf and Lorenge at the opposite end of the range.

Left: May Hill, seen from Chase End, the most southerly of the Malvern Hills.

*Between the Black Mountains in the West and the Severn estuary to the south, lies the
extensive area of the Forest of Dean. Here, wild boar are once again well-established
having been absent since about 1260, when they were probably the last in the country.
Potentially a dangerous animal if cornered, they are in fact secretive in their
habits, requiring large tracts of forest in which to disappear. The industrialisation of the
forests, rather than hunting, was probably the cause of their demise.*

The Severn, is Britain's longest river and also has the second highest tidal range in the world. This photograph shows the Severn looping its way over the flat Vale of Berkeley towards the sea. Great sandbanks are exposed at low tide which attract thousands of wading birds, wildfowl and sea birds.

the 'Dean Forest Mercury'. Questions were asked in Parliament. Following this, a journalist was sent to interview her and reported, 'her hair is tangled and tousled and ragged, grey wisps hanging about her … dirty old face'. He went on to qualify this by writing that she had a merry twinkle in her eye and showed good humour. Ellen was later, in 1906, taken before the court at Littledean, over a pig she was alleged to have been paid to cure. She was charged under the Witchcraft Act of 1735 which prosecuted those pretending to be a witch in order to deceive. The case was dismissed.

The traditional May Day celebrations in May Hill no longer involve a mock battle between armies of youths representing winter and summer, but Morris dancers meet there and are joined by an appreciative crowd of celebrants.

For those who like a more challenging form of entertainment, there is the annual February May Hill Massacre, an 8¾ mile race up 1000 feet of hillside followed by paths through mud, water and woodland, in aid of the Cystic Fibrosis Trust.

The light was fading fast as I walked down the hill to the road. A slow, weary clip-clopping of hooves on the road's metalled surface caused me to pause. A riderless pony appeared over the brow of the hill, which I recognised by its shaggy looks as one of a herd that lives on May Hill. Listlessly, it halted every few steps, coming to a full stop by the gate behind me. Hesitant, it seemed unsure what to do next. Others arrived in ones and twos until there were a dozen or so. One, in a rather desultory way, nibbled at a blade of grass before passing through a gap beside the gate on to the hill where I feared it would find little to eat, the turf having been grazed so heavily that the hill's summit looked more like a bowling green. The rest of the ponies followed, no doubt to spend the night within the shelter of the silver birches and other small deciduous trees that cover that part of the hill.

Among the herd was a brown and white mare with a very young foal, almost completely white with just a couple of small brown patches, like genetic afterthoughts. In a sudden explosion of energy he took off, galloping in a wide circle round and round his mother, who completely ignored him. Unlike the world-weary adults, he was clearly full of the joys of a young life in an equally young spring.

Right: Looking as though it has escaped from a 19th century railway station platform, a cast iron plaque above a fluted column, stands among the fir trees on May Hill's summit, and commemorates Queen Victoria's Jubilee.

Below: May Hill from Dursley Cross. A lively mixture of areas of cleared woodland, houses and blossom-laden fruit trees.

'Nice in summer, but cold and damp in winter' was the response of the woman emerging from the open door of the cottage on May Hill when I complimented her on her pretty cottage and its fine views.

NOTTINGHAM HILL
AND LANGLEY HILL
279 metres ❖ *915 feet*

igher than its neighbour, Langley Hill, by a mere 5 metres (16.5 feet), Nottingham Hill looks west across the Severn valley, while Langley Hill looks north towards Evesham and east along the Cotswold escarpment. Not in itself the most interesting of hills, with its ovoid shape and flat top, Nottingham Hill is nevertheless a good vantage point from which to view nearby Oxenton Hill, Bredon Hill and Alderton Hill, and the most distant, Malvern hills. Having navigated my way up a muddy bridleway from Gotherington station, and round water-filled hoof prints to reach the summit, I was content to sit and enjoy this scenery and watch the steam trains chugging past Gotherington far below.

Until the 1850s twin stones are said to have stood on Nottingham Hill called Odo and Dodo, commemorating two dukes of Mercia. Brothers of that name are reputed to have founded a church at Tewkesbury in 715 on the site now occupied by the abbey.

The river Isbourne separates Langley Hill from West Down and Cleeve Common, part of the broad mass of the Cotswold hills. The escarpment here has many indentations, green and fertile valleys descending to the river. On a promontory between two of these valleys, Belas Knap, a longbarrow for the dead, was erected 5,000 years or so ago by early colonisers of these islands where it stood as a landmark visible from below and from Salter's Hill opposite.

Three thousand years later, a Roman, perhaps a retired legionnaire, built himself a villa a little lower down the hillside, below the longbarrow.

At the foot of these hills, in the valley beside the Isbourne, lies Winchcombe, a town dating back at least as far as the tenth century AD. Its name, in fact, derives from the river and an early settler, 'Esa's stream'.

An abbey was founded at Winchcombe by King Coenwulf at the start of the 9th century as a suitable site for the mausoleum of the Mercian royal family, one of its earliest occupants being the king's martyred son, Saint Kenelm. The legend grew that Kenelm had been murdered by his older sister and his tutor when he was seven years old, in order to gain the throne. The body had been buried at Clent under a thorn bush. The deed became known to the Pope in Rome when a white dove alighted on the high altar in St Peter's, carrying in its beak a message written on parchment. The body was exhumed and carried to Winchcombe by the monks. At each stopping place along the way a spring of water miraculously appeared, the last of which may be seen on Salter's Hill just north of the road from Winchcombe to Guiting Power. This legend improved the town's prosperity, attracting pilgrims from far and wide right up to the time of the Dissolution of the Monasteries 700 years later. Unfortunately, there is very little truth in the legend. Although there was a King Kenelm who in all probability was buried at Winchcombe, his sister, Quenryth, was a respected abbess of Southminster, who in 824 was disputing land ownerships with the Archbishop of Canterbury.

By the late 10th century, Winchcombe had become an important fortified town and administrative centre for its own county, Winchcombeshire, with twelve separate hundreds and a mint. The Old Mint House still exists at 8 Hailes Street. In the following century there were ten mills operating in the locality and a further six in the manor of Sudeley.

Opposite: The Malvern Hills from near Manor Farm, Nottingham Hill.

The present church of St Peter in Winchcombe was built entirely in the Perpendicular style between 1458 and 1468. A golden weathercock surmounts the tower and a frieze of grotesque gargoyles surrounds the building. One, a fierce moustachioed head, is thought to represent Ralph Boteler, the church's benefactor.

116

Right: The Old Mint House, number 8 Hailes Street, is built on the site of Winchcombe's Saxon mint.

The abbey had acquired over 23,000 acres of land and by the start of the 11th century had begun to rebuild using stone quarried at Monks Holes on Langley Hill. The rebuilding of the abbey church was completed in 1239. The monks had a monopoly of the production and sales of wool and the following years saw increasing profits. In 1485, 2,900 sheep were sheared resulting in 200 fleeces, many of them bought by Italian dealers. Apart from a few people in specialised trades, most people in the town and surrounding district were involved in wool production and arable farming, some working in fulling mills and the well-established cloth industry.

Earlier, in 1251, a Cistercian abbey had been established at Hailes, two miles to the east of Winchcombe. Its unique attraction was a phial containing the blood of Jesus, authenticated by the Patriarch of Jerusalem, later known as Pope Urban IV. At first, the monks at Winchcombe viewed Hailes as competition but it soon became evident that pilgrims visited first the shrine of St Kenelm at Winchcombe before continuing along the pilgrim route to Hailes, so both abbeys benefitted.

During this long period of prosperity, the town's church, dedicated to Saint Peter, had been falling into decay owing to a dispute between the townspeople and the abbey about who was responsible for repairs. It was eventually demolished in the mid 15th century and rebuilt in the Perpendicular style with funds supplied by Rafe Boteler, Lord Sudeley.

The fortunes of both the abbeys at Winchcombe and Hailes came to a shuddering halt in December 1539 when on subsequent days both were forced to surrender all they possessed to Henry VIII's commissioners. The loss of the pilgrims and the abbey's patronage was an economic blow to the town from which it did not recover for many years. However, it now had its first grammar school, established a few years before the Dissolution with a bequest from a legacy of the widow of the town constable, Lady Joan Huddleston. A second gram-

mar school was built in 1621 using masonry from the demolished abbey, by Thomas Seymour of Sudeley Castle. He had married the widow of Henry VIII, Catherine Parr, who died in childbirth at the castle in 1548. Following charges of dishonesty, Thomas was executed and the estate passed to Sir John Bridges, Lord Chandos.

Tobacco cultivation, rather surprisingly, promised a revival of the town's fortunes until its suppression by law in 1619 in order to support the Virginia settlers across the Atlantic.

At the start of the 17th century, Winchcombe's population was a mere 1,000 or so, a third of whom were involved in agriculture and a further quarter in cloth making and allied trades.

Lord Chandos backed the losing side in the civil wars of 1642 to 1651, for which he was penalised by losing a tenth of the value of his estate. In addition, the castle's fortifications were demolished and for the next two hundred years it remained a ruin. The town continued to decline.

In 1837 the Sudeley estate and castle were bought by John and William Dent, a family that proved to be significant benefactors to Winchcombe. Following their deaths, the estate passed to John Dent, their nephew, and his wife Emma. The Dent family were responsible for the erection of new buildings and the repair of old ones in the town, having first rebuilt the castle and applied themselves to the well-being of the estate. They built almshouses and a new infants school and schoolhouse. In 1897, Emma, by then a widow, enlarged buildings bought by the family for a National School so that it could accommodate 170 older girls leaving the infant school. Concerned about drunkenness in the town, she decided to persuade everyone to drink coffee instead of beer. It is, sadly, not reported what the patrons of the town's nineteen inns thought of this development.

Emma Dent's last years were clouded by hostility, some of it political, between herself and the townspeople. She, as one would expect, was a convinced Tory, making her views known to the town, even to the point of sacking a man engaged on rebuilding work at the castle for daring to express views contrary to her own in support of Gladstone and the Liberals. Parish pump politics descended into farce when she was accused of stealing the town stocks and keeping them in the castle. She died aged 76 in 1900.

Winchcombe has suffered three significant reversals of fortune in its history. The first, the dissolution of the monastery, next the suppression of its burgeoning tobacco agriculture and finally Lord Chandos's financial penalties following the Royalists defeat in the Civil War. Like other towns that have failed to grow, this has probably been a blessing to the town's present population, who enjoy its streets of attractive and historic shops and houses, most of it a conservation area. Sudeley Castle welcomes visitors who, perhaps like their pilgrim forebears, continue up the road to visit the ruins of Hailes Abbey. A few may even choose to walk through fields of grazing cattle and sheep along the Pilgrim's way, now known as the Cotswold Way.

Left: Busy Hailes Street, the medieval road to Hailes Abbey. Many of the houses in the town are timber-framed but were later given stone 'make-overs' at the front.

Pictured above is North Street which, together with Hailes Street and High Street, led to the crossroads at the heart of the town.
A lane which was a continuation of North Street once led directly to the ford in the river Isbourne but it had gone by 1500.

Above: Vineyard Street descends a hill to cross the river Isbourne over a bridge that replaced a ford. This south-facing slope suited the cultivation of the abbey's grapes.

Below: Jacobean House, built in 1618 to house the King's School, had rooms on the first floor, with a separate entrance for the master.

Below: The Chandos Almshouses, built in 1573 and rebuilt in 1841.

Left: St Kenelm's Well, on the hillside south of Winchcombe, is believed to be the last resting place of the body of the murdered young king before it was carried down to the town for burial.

Below: Winchcombe in its sheltered valley below Salters Hill, and Sudeley Hill, along the top of which is the route of an ancient saltway.

Opposite right: Cleeve Hill, from Nottingham Hill, overlooks Cheltenham and the broad Severn plain.

Left: The green lane crossing the plateau of Nottingham Hill has been colonised by field scabious and in late summer these lilac-blue button-shaped flowers are sufficient reward in themselves for the climb to the summit.

Above: Bishops Cleeve, seen from Nottingham Hill.

Left: The woolly thistle, rare in most of England but common in parts of the Midlands, where, as here on Nottingham Hill, it grows in densely concentrated colonies.

Above: Horsetail is a very ancient and primitive plant with a creeping rootstock. It is attractive in the wild, but unwelcome to most gardeners for whom it can become a pernicious weed.

Left: Trees covering the escarpment at the top of Langley Hill.

Above: This little patch of germander speedwell was growing on Langley Hill at the top where the field meets the wooded escarpment. Isolated clumps of this plant are relatively common, and its little bright blue flowers invariably brighten their surroundings, a welcome surprise to the walker. Worn by travellers, the plant was believed to speed them on their journey.

Slipping and sliding my way down a muddy path that descends the tree-covered hilltop escarpment of Langley Hill and with my eyes fixed on my feet as I inched my way through a jungle of undergrowth that hid from my view the countless exposed tree roots snaking across the track, I was startled, on briefly looking up, to see looming out of the shadows of the trees, the somewhat ghostly silhouette of a large white cow, fixing me with that melancholy stare that is a peculiarity of bovines. As I walked from glade to glade at the foot of the escarpment, other cows appeared, all seeking shade from the heat of the midday sun. The large herd that can often be found there during the summer months barely registered a flicker of interest as I passed among them.

Until a few generations ago, village entertainment, especially for men, seems to have involved fighting and broken heads. It was not uncommon for neighbouring villages to cherish ancient grievances, leading to pitched battles from time to time. Games also involved bare fist boxing and fighting with sticks and cudgels. Shin-kicking contests were very popular, too. A feud of this kind existed between Bishop's Cleeve and Woodmancote, and between Woolstone and Gotherington. Roy Palmer, in his 'Folklore of Gloucestershire', tells of a Winchcombe man who came home from Gretton Wake with his head 'all bloodied' from a backsword fight. Without a word, his father reached up to a shelf, took down a cudgel and strode out. Later, having walked to Gretton and back, he returned, replaced the cudgel and said, 'I've broke his arm'.

Opposite right: Langley Hill, from Dixton Hill, its wooded escarpment at the summit clearly visible.

QUILIBET IN TEMPESTATE PORTUS
(Harbour in a storm for whoever wishes).
Few roadside shelters invite the traveller, in Latin, to take cover from the rain. This
otherwise very rustic-looking hut stands beside the road between
Gretton and Dixton Hill.

Prescott Speed Hill Climb

The Prescott Speed Hill Climb on the northern slopes of Nottingham Hill is the home of 'The Bugatti Owners' Club' and has been so since 1937 when Eric and Godfrey Giles, Secretary and Chairman of the Club, bought the Prescott estate and granted a lease to the Club for a nominal rent. Work began immediately to improve the muddy farm track up the hill to the house and to construct a return road, erect fences and remove some of the trees. The project was completed in time for a full programme of events for the 1938 season.

Since then, the course has been lengthened from 880 to 1127 yards, a distance covered in a breathtaking 36 seconds by some modern cars. It is no longer necessary to own a Bugatti to be a member of the club which currently has 1750 members, including 500 from overseas.

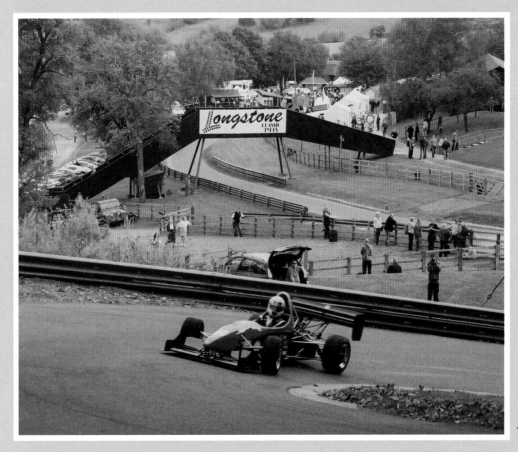

Rounding Pardon Hairpin, with the starting point and facilities in the background.

The viewing public has unrestricted access, including the paddocks, where competitors can be seen with their cars, anxiously making final adjustments, or in some cases, more radical changes. The wives, partners and girlfriends meanwhile picnic behind on the grass, keeping half an eye on their toddlers and small children, a few of whom no doubt are already aspiring grease monkeys as they race in and out of the lines of high powered, temperamental, brightly-coloured machines, all vying for attention as much as any diva.

These photographs were all taken at the last event of the 2009 season, 'The Autumn Classic'.

A selection of photographs, including cars from the past, a few dismantled competitors' cars, with missing wheels and components scattered around, whilst others gleam in the sunshine beside their proud owners.

*A lovingly preserved and polished MG open sports car from the past,
parked away from the action in the shade of trees.*

OXENTON HILL

223 metres ❖ *734 feet*

From the village of Oxenton there is a choice of two footpaths over the hill. One is part of the Gloucestershire Way, and goes south to Woolstone and east to Dixton Hill. The other heads north to Teddington. The latter is only a mile or so in length but packs a lot into that short distance, passing through mixed habitats of hillside fields, woodland where I surprised a young fox, and patches of chest-high bracken, before descending to Teddington. On a clear day many of the hills featured in the pages of this book are visible, May Hill, the Malvern hills, Abberley and Woodbury Hills and in the far distance, the two Clee hills. Nearest, and to the north, lies Bredon Hill. Tewkesbury Abbey is just a few miles to the west and, given an exceptionally clear day, even Gloucester Cathedral is just visible down the Severn valley. The other footpath, going south over Crome Hill to Woolstone, reveals the Nottingham and Langley hills and the Cotswold escarpment sweeping southwards.

   Apart from these two footpaths and one other to Alstone, Oxenton Hill is without paths, even lacking a Right of Way to the summit, a fact that made me think twice before including it. However, the hill has two overwhelming assets in its favour. 'Dixton Harvesters' and 'Dixton Manor' are a pair of very large paintings by an unknown artist that are part of Cheltenham Art Gallery and Museum's collection. They were commissioned around 1730 by Squire Higford of Dixton Manor which is situated on a little hill at the eastern end of

The modern photographs, shown for comparison, were taken on or near the spot from where the artist viewed the harvest scene, and are remarkable for showing how little has changed in the last 180 years. Allowing for the artist's deliberate exaggeration of some of the landscape features, many of the fields are little changed in size and shape. Even the curved track on the right appears to be where it was nearly three centuries ago. Agriculture, however, has changed. It is now highly mechanised and no longer labour intensive as the empty fields in the modern photographs clearly, and perhaps poignantly, show. Most of the population now live and work in the towns and cities.

Dixton Harvesters circa 1725
Copyright: Cheltenham Art Gallery and Museums
The Bridgeman Art Library Limited.

Oxenton Hill, and inexplicably becomes Woolstone Hill on the south side.

'Dixton Harvesters' shows hay being harvested. A line of men scythe the grass, women and girls rake it up and boys fork it into heaps. The hay is then loaded onto horse-drawn wagons. The workers are being entertained by musicians with instruments, as a line of Morris dancers enter the scene at the bottom right. The companion painting in the gallery, 'Dixton Manor', like this one, is full of incident, but principally shows the squire and his family at the door of Dixton Manor, receiving visitors who have arrived in a handsome black coach drawn by a pair of black horses. Like the 'Dixton Harvesters', it depicts the extent of the squire's estate. 'All this is mine' the paintings proclaim.

Below: Oxenton Hill viewed from near Alstone, the wooded, northern aspect of the hill.

Right: The gentle slope of Oxenton Hill descends to Oxenton village and the Severn plain.

Right: From the left, Crane Hill, Oxenton Hill and Dixton Hill, seen from Langley Hill.

A field of barley on Dixton Hill, yet to ripen before it can be harvested.

Right: Ceonothus in full flower in the garden of a thatched timber-framed cottage in Oxenton.

Below: The track to the summit of Oxenton Hill, unfortunately not a right-of-way.

Below: The village of Oxenton, amidst a regular grid of well-tended fields, and with its church at the end of the road, beneath the hill.

Below: Teddington and Bredon Hill from Oxenton Hill. St Nicholas' church in the village has a chancel arch which has been compared to that in the Saxon church at Deerhurst, near Tewkesbury. The church, however, seems to have lost its medieval village and is surrounded by modern houses.

Right: St Nicholas' pulpit dates from Cromwell's time and bears the names of the churchwardens in 1655.

Below: The little church at Alstone, guarded by a topiary peacock.

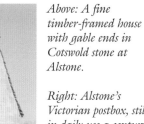

Above: A fine timber-framed house with gable ends in Cotswold stone at Alstone.

Above: Timber-framed Alstone cottages with a rather grand one on the end in Cotswold stone.

Right: Alstone's Victorian postbox, still in daily use a century after it was installed, and looking as though it might last into the next century. In 1840 stamps were stuck on letters which had to be posted at post offices until letter boxes were erected in the streets, and by the late 19th century some towns enjoyed up to six deliveries a day.

Two well-established clumps of flag iris or yellow flag, grow in a ditch near Teddington beside the footpath from Oxenton. Also called 'segg' from the Anglo-Saxon for short sword – a reference to the shape of the leaves. The flowers are said to be the source for the fleur-de-lys symbol of French royalty.

Gloucestershire Warwickshire Railway

There is nothing like a railway and, in particular, steam engines, for exciting the imagination and enthusiasm of British men, a fact exemplified by the small group of volunteers who took on the task of rebuilding this line. A heroic achievement! The route hugs the foot of the Cotswold escarpment between Broadway and Cheltenham with stations at Toddington, Winchcombe and Gotherington, but was closed in 1977 with the track dismantled two years later. Even the platforms and buildings at some of the stations were demolished. All had to be rebuilt by the volunteers who are well on their way to achieving their ambition. Trains now, once again, carry passengers between Toddington and Cheltenham racecourse. Timetables show a regular service in summer and winter, with additional special events throughout the year.

In 2009 the BBC's drama series 'Land Girls' about the Women's Land Army during World War II was filmed partly at Toddington Station, which apart from the removal of a few 'no smoking' signs, required no alterations as an authentic station of the period.

This, the longest rebuilt standard gauge heritage railway in the country, which passes through a quintessentially English landscape, is proving to be an outstanding railway rescue success story.

'Black Prince', at Toddington station, the very epitome of steam power.

Right: An historic photograph of Toddington in 1981 shows a forlorn-looking station, its track ripped up and tall weeds growing on the platform next to the booking office. This modern photograph illustrates the scale of achievement since then.

Right: An engine returns from the front to the back of the train at Toddington Station to be ready for the next service to Cheltenham.

Above: Milk churns on a trolley at Winchcombe Station.

Right: This charming little yellow hut with more than a hint of Wendy house about it, is at Toddington station, by the footbridge.

Right: An embankment between Gretton and Gotherington.

Left: Gotherington Halt is owned privately by a railway enthusiast who converted the station for use as his home.

Right: Passenger Information board at Toddington Station.

Gotherington, a halt now, is a credit to its station master/gardener owner.

BREDON HILL
AND ALDERTON HILL
223 metres ❖ *964 feet*

evern's wide valley in the south, the Midland plain to the north, the Malvern hills to the west and the Cotswold escarpment to the east – these are the timeless vistas that reward any who climb to Bredon's summit. The hill is, in effect, a little piece of alien terrain that has escaped into Worcestershire, an island left behind by the Cotswolds slipping away eastwards and, like amber gemstones sewn on the hem of a voluminous crinoline, its dome-shaped hill is encircled by honeycoloured limestone villages. The houses and cottages, sometimes built entirely of limestone but often partly of limestone with timber-framed additions are, almost without exception, picturesque. Bredon, Bredons Norton, Great and Little Comberton, Elmley Castle, Ashton-under-Hill, Beckford, Overbury and Kemerton all have fine churches, some of which, like Bredon and Elmley Castle, contain treasurers that frequently appear as photographs in the glossy pages of books and magazines.

Remarkable aerial photographs of crop marks in a field at Nafford beside the river Avon show concentric circles of a Henge that dates from approximately 3,000 BC, some of the earliest evidence that we have of human activity around Bredon Hill. Clear evidence of later Iron Age activity can be seen on Bredon Hill's highest point, where earthwork fortifications survive. Myths and legends persist, associated with two separate stone outcrops a little over a mile apart. First, the Banbury Stones, in a hollow of the summit, are said to go down to

Above: Cattle at Deerpark Hall.

Opposite right: Deerpark Hall and Bredon Hill. The tower was erected near to the hill's summit within the Iron Age fortifications that dominate the hill's highest ground. Evidence for an even earlier occupation of the hill occurred when Bronze Age Beaker burials were excavated in the 1960s. A rock-cut grave was discovered containing a male and female skeleton along with two Bronze Age Bell beakers and some arrow heads, a flint scraper and a bone pin.

Left: The graveyard of Bricklehampton church is full of snowdrops, the result, I am told, of years of dividing clumps and transplanting by a patient parishioner who lives nearby.

Below: Eckington bridge, built in 1728-9, sits on 15th century stone piers that originally supported a timber structure. The stone was not quarried locally but transported from a quarry near Ombersley, many miles away.

Above: The Banbury Stone, which is composed of oolite rubble cemented by calcium-rich water, has down the centuries attracted folklore and superstitions. Kissing the stone on Good Friday was thought to bring good luck and it was reputed to have healing properties, but most fanciful of all, the stone was said to go to the river Avon for a drink when the bells of Pershore Abbey were rung.

Right: This simple, attractive topograph, mounted on the surface of a natural rock on the summit of Bredon Hill, is easily missed by those eager to see the views from the edge of the escarpment.

Sunset on the summit of Bredon Hill.

Right: The bewildering variety of gate fastenings in the hills could provide happy hunting for an enthusiastic collector.

Above: A hedge in winter, decorated with the white, fluffy seedheads of traveller's joy, also called 'old man's beard'.

Right: Woods in winter, along the edge of Bredon Hill's north-facing escarpment.

Right: Two Cotswold outliers, Bredon Hill and Alderton Hill, seen from the Cotswold escarpment. Until the arrival of the Romantic movement, travellers regarded uplands everywhere with fear and foreboding. In the early 19th century the Cotswolds were described by one traveller as 'one of the most unfortunate, desolate countries under heaven … abandoned to the screaming kites and larcenous crows'.

Right: Bredon Church's celebrated alabaster memorial to Sir Giles Reed who died in 1611, and his wife Catherine Greville, daughter of Sir Fulke Greville, the great Warwickshire landowner. Once an ecclesiastical centre, a monastery was founded here in about 716 by Eanulph and was endowed by his grandson, King Offa. Basically a Norman church, it has a very unusual and striking north porch.

Below: Unique in Worcestershire, Bredon's 13th century tithe barn has aisles and two porches, one with an upper room containing a fireplace.

the river Avon to drink when a church clock strikes midnight, and on Good Friday people used to climb the hill to kiss the stones. Secondly, the King and Queen stones on the escarpment above Westmancote were, until the end of the 18th century, whitewashed annually in preparation for a session of the manorial court. Up to the end of the 19th century people were passed between the stones as a cure for their ailments.

The chancel of Bredon church contains the grave of Bishop Prideaux, who experienced hard times during the Commonwealth, and retired to Bredon on a pittance of 4s 6d (22.5p) a week. In 'Historic Worcestershire' by W Salt Brassington, published in 1894, a conversation is recorded between the bishop and a friend he encountered on his way to the blacksmith with some old iron. He was taking it in order to raise 7d (nearly 3p) to buy his dinner. The friend asked how he fared. 'Never better in my life', the bishop answered, 'only I have too great a stomach; for I have eaten the little plate which the sequestrators left me; I have eaten a great library of excellent books; I have eaten a great deal of linen, much of my brass, some of my pewter and I am now come to eat my iron, and what will come next, I know not'.

Bredon's name, like the hills, is derived from the Celtic 'bre' and the Saxon 'dun', making it, in effect, 'HillHill'. The church was built between the 12th and 14th centuries on the site of a Saxon church destroyed by Danish invaders in the mid-9th century. There is also a 13th century tithe barn with aisles and two porches, one with an upper room and fireplace. The 17th century almshouses were founded by descendents of Sir Giles and Lady Catherine Reed, whose fine alabaster and black marble monument can be seen in the church.

The name of the village, Elmley Castle, ie 'the woodland clearing among elm trees' describes the site of the long-gone medieval castle that once stood there. It was built by

Opposite left: The King and Queen Stones on Bredon Hill's steep west-facing escarpment.

Left: The Fox and Hounds in Bredon village.

Below: Viewed from Bredon Hill, the spire of St Giles' church at Bredon is the most conspicuous feature of the flooded Avon valley.

Opposite right: Both the rivers Avon and Severn are prone to annual floods. This photograph shows the M5 motorway crossing the Avon near Bredon. The confluence of the two rivers is just a few miles downstream at Tewkesbury, where flooding sometimes results in serious hardship for many and even death for one or two unfortunate people.

Below left: Bredon Norton's beautiful Manor House dates from 1585. Victoria Woodhull Martin, the only woman until very recently to run for President of the United States of America, lived here in the early 20th century. She published her suffragette beliefs in her own newspaper. Unsurprisingly, her radical views on everything from vegetarianism to prostitution not only failed to win her votes, she was also asked to leave the country.

Left: Carved outlines of hands on a stone bench in the north porch of Little Comberton Church are believed to be those of newly married brides.

Below: St Peter's Church, Little Comberton, stands on a site where Roman pottery, glass and coins have been discovered. It has a tympanum in the north doorway that continues to puzzle commentators – a simple cross surrounded by eight whorls.

Opposite page: Great Comberton and the river Avon, seen from the top of Bredon Hill. 'Magna Cumbritune' in the 13th century, the present day population is little different to that in those earlier times. Quay Lane leads to the river where corn destined for Nafford Mill was loaded on to boats. The mill burned down in 1909.

Elm-laeh, a clearing in an elm wood, is the 8th century name for the village of Elmley Castle, which in 1575 played host to Queen Elizabeth I and her court, a costly business for reluctant hosts and a way of reducing expenditure for the monarch. She was entertained by William Savage in the fine Manor of Elmley, built for the family in 1544, and demolished in 1963 to make way for a housing estate.

Robert Despencer, William the Conqueror's steward. Later it was owned by the Beauchamps who also owned land on more than fifty Worcestershire manors. In the mid 13th century William Beauchamp married the heiress of the Earl of Warwick, and his son assumed the title. The upwardly mobile Beauchamps, destined to become statesmen and military leaders, enlarged and improved the fortifications of Warwick Castle, turning it into the impregnable and mighty edifice we see today. Their former castle at Elmley fell steadily into decline, the stones eventually being carried away for re-use elsewhere, including repairs to the bridge over the Avon at Pershore. The site is now a refuge for violet click beetles, one of only two locations in the country where they are to be found, according to a recent feature in a national newspaper. The click beetle is so-named from its habit of clicking as it springs from an upside down position to a normal one.

Elmley Castle village, far below the site of the castle, is a quiet, largely residential place surrounded by farms. 'Bentley's History, Gazateer and Directory of Worcestershire' from the mid 19th century, records that at that time Elmley Castle had a blacksmith, a miller, a tailor, a shopkeeper, a wheelwright, a schoolmaster, a grocer, a butcher, a wood-turner, a baker, two beer-sellers, eight farmers and five shoemakers. All occupations apart from the schoolmaster and the farmers have, of course, long gone.

Bredon Hill, like many parts of our ancient landscape, has a few well-hidden treasures. St Catherine's Well, a spring at the foot of the hill's highest escarpment which is also the site

The exquisitely carved gilded alabaster memorial in St Mary's Church, Elmley Castle,
commemorates William Savage, who died in 1616, his son Giles
who died in 1631, and his wife Catherine, whose baby clutches a golden purse in
its tiny fist. She died in 1674 and was buried in Great Malvern Priory.
Their four sons are shown kneeling at their feet.

of a Saxon chapel, is one. Another is at Netherton Farm, where the ruins of a Norman chapel contain an astonishing dragon tympanum which has been dated to the period 1175 to 1200. It has been variously interpreted as being derived from the medieval sawfish which spread its wings and chased ships, terrifying their crew, or as an allegorical beast. Bestiaries arrived in England during the early 12th century interpreting animals in terms of Christian morality, either good or bad. The dragon usually represented the Devil, 'who lies in wait for any who stray outside the church … therefore beware all you can lest you are found outside that house and that old dragon catches and devours you'. Dragons were deeply embedded in the medieval consciousness and sculptures of them are commonly found in early Norman churches. Before the Normans, Anglo Saxon kings had used a fierce dragon as their emblem.

Netherton chapel is an evocative ruin in a beautiful setting, the garden of a private farmhouse. Its dragon, still a disturbing and powerful image offers a glimpse into the strange world of the medieval mind.

There are a wide variety of routes up Bredon Hill from almost every village below. One of my current favourites is the footpath that begins at Grafton, a small hamlet of picturesque

The 12th century Dragon tympanum at Netherton Chapel.

Ashton-under-Hill is memorable for its long main street flanked by a harmonious mixture of timber-framed thatched cottages and Cotswold stone houses. The Norman church has an unusual dedication to Saint Barbara, who is reputed to offer protection from lightning strikes. Near the lych gate there stands a medieval stone cross above a three-step base. I always pause to admire the carved letterforms of the stone in the photograph – these are executed with such style and confidence. The stone is inset into the wall of the church near the entrance porch.

Below: Water still flows from the village pump in Grafton.

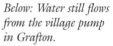

Left and right: Two cottages in Grafton, a small village on the south side of Bredon Hill. 'Norman Cottage' justifies its name when one notices the blocked up Romanesque arch in the gable wall – this was once a Norman church.

old cottages, rises to a hidden green valley enclosed by woodland, then passes a stone barn that was built with the same amount of care as though for human habitation. From there, the path continues to Conderton Hill above an ancient earthworks, followed by a gradual ascent of about a mile-and-a-half to the summit.

Here of a Sunday morning
My love and I would lie,
And see the coloured counties,
And hear the larks so high
About us in the sky.
A E Houseman, 'Bredon Hill'.

Bredon Hill is much the same, I would guess, as in Houseman's time. There may be fewer skylarks, their songs drowned by the constant hum of traffic on the M5 two miles away, but the grassy slopes and shady woods are still there, as are the dry-stone walls enclosing stony fields of waving corn on Bredon's broad plateau.

Below: Grafton on the left of the picture, and Alderton Hill, seen from the lower slopes of Bredon Hill.

Right: Sheep have a reputation for being compliant, docile animals, happiest when left undisturbed to nibble at grass or rest in the shade of a tree. There is another side to their character. If it's possible to get stuck a sheep will do so. Lambs in particular have a talent for getting trapped between fences and impenetrable hedges of blackthorn and hawthorn. Sheep sometimes end up on their backs with their legs pointing skywards, a position which renders them immobile. Farmers tend to become blasé about it, as I discovered when reporting one such encounter to a hill farmer. 'I'll send someone up later' she wearily responded. On Bredon Hill, I recently came across a sheep that at first, I thought was lying down on a cattle grid. But no, it had all four legs in the pit between the bars. It was later rescued by the farmer.

The sheep in the photograph were resting under a tree on the hillside above Grafton from where there is a footpath to the top of Bredon Hill. Like all good hill routes, this one is full of ever-changing landscapes. Beginning at the picturesque village, the path crosses two hillside fields to a narrow belt of trees encircling a hidden valley. The route then heads for the barn in the photographs, from where it follows a broad track towards the top of the escarpment. There it turns left to pass above Conderton Camp, and a track leading to the hill's summit.

This stone barn, left and below, is typical of hundreds in the area constructed with as much care and skill as any house, consequently they are much in demand for barn-conversions.

The four plants featured on this page are but a few of the many species that can be found on Bredon Hill. The woolly thistle, top left, is here shown at the emerging flower-bud stage. For comparison, see the thistle in full flower on page 122.

Below: I know of three colonies of pyramidal orchids on Bredon Hill, no doubt there are others. Over fifty species of orchid grow throughout Britain, varying in size from the 5feet (1.52m) tall lizard orchid, to the 6 inch (15.24cm) tall autumn ladies' tresses. Like many, the pyramidal orchid is found on chalk or lime-rich soils and is said to have a foxy smell, the reason for its attraction to moths. To the touch, the flower cluster feels like the softest velvet.

Left: Wild thyme growing at the highest part of Bredon Hill, enjoying the shelter of a Cotswold stone wall.

Right: St Faith's Church, Overbury, in springtime.

Above: Greater knapweed flourishes on the limestone soil of the hill. Flora Britannica records the occurrence of a single plant with white flowers at nearby Pershore in 1980.

Left: St Faith's Church's lychgate, erected as a war memorial in 1921.

Below: The Norman font in Overbury Church.

Overbury is a particularly pretty village, with a fine 18th century court. Houses and cottages line the long street leading directly up Bredon Hill. 'An excellent stream of water issues out of the hills and turns a few small manufactories, which, finding employment for many of the inhabitants, makes Overbury a thriving village' writes the author of Bentley's 1842 History and Directory of Worcestershire. In the 18th and early 19th centuries, the village had several water mills producing paper, flour and silk thread.

Left: A house in Overbury.

Opposite right: Aubretia and Cotswold stone walls go together like the horse and carriage of the song. The plant thrives on limestone.

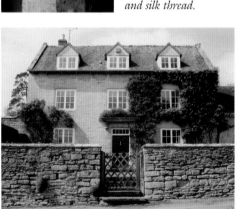

Below: Thatched, timber-framed cottages on Alderton's quiet main street.

Below: Wisteria and clematis beautify an already perfect timber-framed cottage in Alderton.

Alderton Hill and its near-neighbour, Bredon Hill are divided by a county boundary. Alderton is in Gloucestershire, Bredon in Worcestershire. Apart from that, they have much in common. Alderton Hill, though by far the smaller of the two, like its neighbour is encircled by villages of charming old cottages and houses clustering round ancient churches. Some houses are timber-framed, whilst others are built entirely of stone, which is somewhat confusing for the visitor who wonders whether this is part of the leafy world of Worcestershire or the limestone Cotswolds. The answer, of course, is that this is a part of England where the two regions meet.

It is rare these days to find a small village with a shop but Alderton has one and it appears to be thriving, as is the village school where children in neat uniforms play organised games in a walled playground just yards away from passers-by and traffic.

Alderton Hill is well-wooded with mainly deciduous trees belonging to the Dumbleton Estate, for whom the 'right to roam' legislation has clearly not yet arrived, as is shown by a rash of warning yellow 'Keep Out' signs. There are, however, a number of waymarked public footpaths including the Wychavon Way that crosses the hill from north to south.

Yellow gorse, a conspicuous feature of the southern end of triangular-shaped Alderton Hill.

Spring is perhaps the best time of the year to walk in the woods of Alderton Hill, when the bluebells work their magic.

A balloonist drifts with the wind into the sunset over Alderton Hill.

In conclusion

There is little that is unique to this selection of hills, others like them can be found in many regions of the country. It is, indeed, their essential 'Englishness' that is a large part of their charm. Local vernacular architecture tells you where you are, whether in sandstone, limestone, or leafy wooded countryside. Long ago successive waves of migrants and invaders brought new social structures, new cultures, and new religions, but changed the landscape only very slowly – content to leave things as they were. Small patches of forest were cleared and eventually became consolidated but trees were a valuable resource to every local economy, so remained a familiar part of the scene. The biggest upheaval occurred when medieval open-field strip agriculture made way for enclosure, and the farms moved from the villages and towns to the centre of their new fields. The medieval system, however, had prevailed for so long that even now one can walk across ridge and furrow, climb a style in a hedge, and resume the same ridge and furrow in the next field. It is the landscape treasured today by millions and familiar to us all.

The photographs within the pages of this book were obtained by visiting all of the hills in all seasons and all weathers, everything from the balmy days of high summer to the fog, snow and ice of mid-winter. As both walker and photographer I welcome both. Summer may be more congenial, with its long, warm days, but with the sun high in the sky, photographs of landscapes, no matter how promising as subjects, almost inevitably end up as dull, flat-lit pictures. What summer offers, of course, is the rich kaleidoscope of greens and subtle colours of a constantly changing flora. Winter sun, low in the sky, does most of the photographer's work, with the added bonus of sunset at four in the afternoon, a few precious moments when every scene is transformed into a theatrical event. Hanging around in summer until late evening for a sunset that may not happen is not my idea of fun, but then neither, in winter, is fumbling with a camera and tripod, fingers so cold they have lost all feeling.

On a particularly clear day recently, I strolled along the ridgeway near to where I live on the Worcestershire Warwickshire border and for the first time, to my surprise, noticed that every hill featured in this book was visible, strung out along the horizon, from the Clee hills in the north to May Hill in the south. Only Oxenton Hill and Nottingham Hill could not be seen, and that only because they were hidden by Bredon Hill. To the people who live within sight of these hills this is 'home', as it is for me.

John Bradford

BIBLIOGRAPHY

Bentley's History, Directory etc of Worcestershire 1842.

Bowden, Mark, *The Malvern Hills, an ancient landscape.*

Brassington, W Salt, *Historic Worcestershire 1894.*

Bridges, Tim, *Churches of Worcestershire.*

Donaldson, D N, Winchcombe, *A history of the Cotswold borough.*

Hoggard, Brian, Bredon Hill.

Jenkins, A E, *Titterstone Clee Hills. Everyday life, industrial history and dialect.*

Jenkins, Simon, *England's Thousand Best Churches.*

Leonard, John, *Churches of Shropshire and their treasures.*

Mabey, Richard, *Flora Britannica.*

Osborne, Bruce and Weaver, *Cora, Springs, spouts, fountains and holy wells of the Malvern Hills.*

Aquae Malvernsis. *The springs and fountains of the Malvern Hills.*

Palmer, Martin and Nigel, *Sacred Britain.*

Palmer, Roy, *The folklore of Gloucestershire.*

Philips, Roger, *Wild Flowers of Britain.*

Poulton-Smith, Anthony, *Worcestershire placenames.*

Rackham, Oliver, *History of the Countryside.*

Raven, Michael, *A Shropshire Gazateer.*

Standbridge, Steve and Locke, David, *The new GWR. 25 years of the Gloucestershire Warwickshire Railway.*

The Worcestershire Group of the Milestone Society, *Finding Worcestershire Milestones.*

Victoria History of the County of Worcester.

John Bradford, a graphic designer and landscape photographer has lived within sight of nearly all the hills featured in this book and knows the area well, having walked along many of its footpaths, bridleways and lanes. Exploring the English and Welsh

A stone barn at sunset on Bredon Hill.

countryside has been an interest for the last thirty years, during which time he has continually added to his collection of photographs. These have appeared in four previous books, *The river Teme, The river Avon* and *The river Severn*, three books that follow the length of each river, all published by Hunt End Books. A second edition of *The river Severn* is published by Brewin Books Ltd. John's first book, *Worcestershire, a portrait of the county* by Sam Redgrave, is published by Halfshire books.